BRITISH RAILWAYS

PAST and PRESENT

No 17

Lines closed

Lines open

BRITISH RAILWAYS

PAST and PRESENT

No 17
Cornwall

David Mitchell

Past and Present

Past & Present Publishing Ltd

© David Mitchell 1993

First published in May 1993

British Library Cataloguing in Publication Data

A catalogue record for this book is available from the British Library

ISBN 1 85895 001 5

Past & Present Publishing Ltd
Unit 5
Home Farm Close
Church Street
Wadenhoe
Peterborough PE8 5TE
Tel/fax (08015) 4-4-0

All the 'present' photographs in this book were taken by David Mitchell.

Map on page 2 drawn by Christina Siviter

Printed and bound in Great Britain

BURNGULLOW: During the mid-1980s the railways of Cornwall enjoyed a brief period of relative autonomy under the Truro Area Manager. A manifestation of this independence is the headboard adorning Class '37' No 37196. The locomotive had been painted at St Blazey in the new Railfreight livery prior to being named *Tre Pol and Pen* at Truro on 16 July 1985. On 6 September it was coupled with No 37308 and the duo were pictured before taking a china clay train to Carne Point. The massive Blackpool clay works dominates the background while the original Cornwall Railway station was located on the extreme right of this view (see page 107). The engine's name is now carried by one of St Blazey's refurbished Class '37s', No 37671.

**'By Tre, Ros, Pol, Lan, Car and Pen
Ye shall know most Cornishmen.'**

***Title page:* Cornish Railways lizard logo as worn by No 37207 *William Cookworthy*.**

CONTENTS

BIBLIOGRAPHY

...any reader wishes to investigate the railways of Cornwall ... more detail, the following books are suggested, all of ...hich have been referred to in caption research for this ...le:

...he Railways of Cornwall 1809-1963 by C. R. Clinker
...David & Charles)
...rack Layout Diagrams of GWR, Vols 10, 11 and 13
... R. A. Cooke
...tlas of the GWR by R. A. Cooke (Wild Swan)
...he Story of Cornwall's Railways by A. Fairclough (Tor ...ark)
... Regional History of the Railways of Great Britain, Vol 1
...he West Country by David St John Thomas (David & ...harles)
...he GWR in West Cornwall by Alan Bennett (Kingfisher)
...he GWR in Mid Cornwall by Alan Bennett (Kingfisher)
...he GWR in East Cornwall by Alan Bennett (Runpast)
...he Branch Lines of Cornwall by Lewis Reade (Atlantic)
...ranch Line Memories - Great Western by Lewis Reade ...Atlantic)

Branch Line Memories - Southern by Lewis Reade (Atlantic)
The Newquay Branch and its Branches by John Vaughan (OPC)
An Illustrated History of West Country China Clay Trains by John Vaughan (OPC)
Diesels in the Duchy by John Vaughan (Ian Allan)
Caradon & Looe by M. J. Messenger (Twelveheads Press)
The Withered Arm by T. W. E. Roche (Forge Books)
Atlantic Coast Express by S. Austin (Ian Allan)
The Bude Branch by D. J. Wroe (Kingfisher)
Callington Railways by R. Cromblehome, B. Gibson, D. Stuckey and C. Whetmath (Forge Books)
The Bodmin & Wadebridge Railway by C. F. D. Whetmath (Town & Country)
Bodmin & Wadebridge 1834-1978 by A. Fairclough and A. Wills (Bradford Barton)
And various issues of the following:
The Railway Observer (Journal of the Railway Correspondence & Travel Society)
Branch Line News (Newsletter of the Branch Line Society)

TRURO SHED: The Cornwall Railway erected an engine shed of timber construction to the north of the station, but this was closed in May 1900 when a new depot was opened to the east of Highertown Tunnel; part of the hills had to be cut away to create the new site. The depot is pictured on 15 May 1959 with a variety of locomotives display. *Mike Mensing*

The shed closed to steam in September 1962, with total closure in November 1965. After demolition, warehousing was erected on the site and one of these units now handles the westernmost revenue-earning freight traffic the Duchy. The 6V35 17.12 (SuO) Ince & Elton-Truro runs as required to deliver Kemira fertiliser to this depot. The author had made two previous trips to photograph this train before finally recording it on a misty 28 September 1992. Class '47' No 47231 *The Silcock Express* shunts empty wagons before its 12.38 return north.

INTRODUCTION

A peninsula largely separated from Devon and the rest of England by the River Tamar, Cornwall is probably the most distinctive county in the country. Its isolation has helped to foster an independent spirit among its inhabitants, not least in their celebration of Celtic traditions and the revival of their own language.

The mining of tin, copper and lead in the county dates from before Roman times, but activity reached a peak in the 18th and 19th centuries when the development of the steam engine and pump enabled workers to go deeper underground. A notable pioneer who did much to develop steam power was Richard Trevithick, who was born in Camborne in 1771. Most of Cornwall's early railways were constructed to carry ore, but their lives were relatively short as cheaper production methods in other counties led to the gradual closure of most mines.

With the opening of the Cornwall Railway in 1859 this isolated land was finally linked to the rest of the country, and the event aided the fishing and farming industries which were now able to send their catches and produce further afield. More importantly in the long run, the arrival of the railway encouraged visitors to travel to this land of mystery and legend, with its variety of attractions including both a mild climate and a magnificent coastline.

Most railway development within the Duchy was initiated by local people, but by the turn of the century the Great Western Railway had acquired the majority of the lines and was to dominate the scene thereafter. Although the London & South Western Railway had purchased the Bodmin & Wadebridge in 1846, it was to be almost 50 years before this line was linked to the rest of its system, and the company's influence was accordingly limited to the north of the county.

The railway network was largely complete by the early years of this century and other than for certain improvements no great changes took place until the 1960s, a decade that was to see the closure of many of Cornwall's stations and much of its track mileage. Three branches were closed prior to the publication of the Beeching Plan, and that report sounded the death knell for most of the others. Fortunately, however, the county fared a little better than certain other parts of British Railways, and the Looe, St Ives and truncated Callington branches were all reprieved. Along with the Newquay and Falmouth branches, they still perform a valuable service to their communities and provide a link to the outside world via the main line and its HST service to London and the north.

Historically the railway has been closely associated with the development of the china clay industry. Although many of the clay lines have now closed, Railfreight activity in Cornwall is currently almost totally dependent on this traffic, and a large tonnage is still carried either for export or to customers in the north. This business has contributed to the survival of the railway in the Duchy and hopefully will continue to do so for many years to come.

However, the future for Cornwall's railway system is presently unclear. InterCity has indicated its desire to electrify the Paddington to Penzance route early in the 21st

century, but recently it has been announced that this will form part of one of the fir
franchises to be offered under the Government's privatisation plans. It remains to
seen how this misconceived programme will proceed, but there has to be a very re
fear that at the very least it might result in through trains terminating at Plymouth.

Once again my thanks are extended to those individuals who kindly allowed m
access to their private property to enable some of the present-day views to be take
My gratitude must also go to the 'past' photographers for providing the archive mat
rial; this book would not have been possible without their foresight and assistance.
has been particularly pleasant for me to study their work as I was growing up in
Austell during the period when most of these photographs were taken. Their camer
have not only recorded scenes that I missed, partly through youthful ignorance, b
have also helped me relive those distant but lingering memories - St Blazey and th
first ever shed-bash; watching the Fowey 'auto' at Golant one evening; cabbing N
41320 at Bodmin North; crossing the Royal Albert Bridge behind a 'Hall' and looki
down at the Tamar below. . .

**David Mitche
Exet**

Great Western in East Cornwall

ROYAL ALBERT BRIDGE, SALTASH (1): The River Tamar acts as a natural boundary between the counties of Cornwall and Devon, and its bridging provided a formidable obstacle to the Cornwall Railway in its plans to link the two ports of Falmouth and Plymouth. In an original scheme provision was made for the trains to cross the river by way of a ferry at Torpoint. However, following Isambard Kingdom Brunel's appointment as engineer, a revised route up-river included the building of a bridge at Saltash, which is pictured here on 2 May 1959, the centenary of its official opening. The fireman of 'Grange' Class 4-6-0 No 6845 *Paviland Grange*, which is working a down goods train, is just about to hand over the single line staff as the engine completes its crossing. *Hugh Ballantyne*

The present scene shows HST power car No 43149 entering Saltash station with the 15.35 Paddington-Penzance on 21 August 1992.

ROYAL ALBERT BRIDGE, SALTASH (2): At this point the Tamar is 1,100 feet wide and 80 feet deep at its maximum and before construction the Admiralty insisted that the bridge had a clear headway above high water of 100 feet. Brunel's design allowed for the constuction of 17 masonry piers, ten of which were on the Cornish side, with two arched wrought iron trusses. These are each of 445 feet span and are carried in mid-stream on a cast iron pier. Due to ill health, Brunel was not able to attend the official opening by the Prince Consort on 2 May 1859, but he was subsequently able to inspect his final masterpiece before his death in September of that year. Although certain modification and strengthening work has been undertaken since, the basic structure still performs satisfactorily today, although the background scene was to change with the building of an adjacent road bridge. This second view, taken on 4 August 1960, clearly shows the work in progress. 'County' Class 4-6-0 No 1023 *County of Oxford* is crossing with a Paddington to Newquay train. *Hugh Ballantyne*

On 13 October 1992 we get a clearer sight of this magnificent structure as 'Sprinter' unit No 158869 crosses with a Swindon to Penzance service.

DEFIANCE PLATFORM: A halt was constructed above Wearde Quay by the men of HMS *Defiance*, a nearby torpedo training school, and was opened in 1905. However, the creation of a double-track deviation line from Saltash to St Germans required the building of a new station, which was opened in 1908. Although closed on 27 October 1930, evidence of the platforms remains on 25 July 1959 as 'Grange' Class 4-6-0 No 6828 *Trellech Grange* passes with the 11.10 pm (Fridays only) Manchester-Penzance. The loop line on the right follows the formation of the original main line. Note the shipping in the right background. *Peter Gray*

The loop was taken out of use in 1965, although part remained as a siding until 1972. On 13 October 1992 Class '37' No 37412 passes with a load of china clay bound for export via Fowey Docks. The train has originated at Marsh Mills on the remaining stub of the erstwhile Tavistock branch.

WEARDE: The 1908 deviation wa
built to replace a single-line section
of the original Cornwall Railway,
which included five timber
viaducts. The new route followed
an inland course with easier grad
ents, reduced track curvature and
only three viaducts. On 4 March
1962 'County' 4-6-0 No 1004 *County
of Somerset* takes the 'new' align
ment with the down 'Cornish
Riviera Express'. The carriage sid
ing leading off to the right was laid
on the formation of the old route.
Wearde signal box can also be
seen. *Terry Nicholls*

The box closed on 31 October
1965 when the carriage siding
were also taken out of use. The
equivalent view of 13 October 199.
shows an HST unit on the 7.5.
Penzance-Edinburgh, the 'Cornish
Scot'. The power cars are No
43065 and 43084.

ST GERMANS (I): On 16 July 1956 'Hall' 4-6-0 No 5943 *Elmdon Hall* passes the station with an up parcels train. The signal box is pictured clearly on the left, whilst the goods yard, complete with its shed, is located behind the photographer. The yard occupies the site of the original 1859 Cornwall Railway alignment. *R. C. Riley*

The signal box closed on 6 May 1973 and was subsequently demolished, its equipment being transferred to a building on the down platform which now acts as the interface between the Plymouth panel and Liskeard signal box. The goods yard was taken out of use in 1965. On 13 September 1992 'Sprinter' No 158825 stands in the down platform with the 7.35 Bristol-Penzance.

ST GERMANS (2): This was one of the original stations when the broad gauge Cornwall Railway opened for traffic from Plymouth Millbay to Truro on 4 May 1859. The station was constructed on a reverse curve and is pictured on 16 July 1956 as 'County' 4-6-0 No 1018 *County of Leicester* speeds through with an up Penzance working. First introduced in 1945, Hawksworth's 'Counties' were regular performers in the Duchy until the end of steam. *R. C. Riley*

The station is still largely intact but the overbridge has lost its roof and the up side buildings are in commercial use. Passing through on a damp 13 September 1992, HST power car No 43033 heads the 8.40 Penzance-Paddington.

MENHENIOT is pictured on 16 July 1956 as 'Castle' Class 4-6-0 No 5023 *Brecon Castle* storms through with the 10.30 Paddington-Penzance, the 'Cornish Riviera Limited'. The train would probably have been worked as far as Plymouth by a 'King' Class locomotive, but due to weight restrictions this type was barred from crossing the Saltash Bridge. Menheniot is located just over 5 miles from St Germans and was similarly constructed on a reverse curve. Behind the photographer on the down side are sidings serving Clicker Tor Quarry; these opened on 7 May 1931 and at one time provided ballast for the railway. *R. C. Riley*

On 15 October 1992 'Sprinter' No 158836 passes through with the 9.14 Plymouth to Penzance service. In the then current timetable five down and three up trains stopped here on weekdays.

Both of these photographs were taken from the footbridge but show a slightly different view due to the bridge's relocation a short distance westwards in the intervening years. The main station buildings have been demolished, and while the quarry is still open, unfortunately the sidings were taken out of use in 1969.

LISKEARD (1): This important town was served by the Cornwall Railway from its opening. The station is depicted here on Saturday 23 May 1959 as 'Hall' 4-6-0 No 4922 *Enville Hall* drifts through with a relief train bound for Birmingham. The line was originally single track although crossing loops were provided at each of the stations; doubling was not to take place until after the abolition of the Broad Gauge in May 1892. Subsequently the track westwards from here to Doublebois was doubled from 4 February 1894, whilst the line eastwards was altered from 9 August 1896. *Michael Mensing*

Liskeard is still an important railhead and today's equivalent view shows Class '153' unit No 153370 calling with the 10.25 Penzance to Plymouth on 13 October 1992.

LISKEARD (2): The station possessed two goods yards, one at each end of the layout. The yard and shed at the west end are shown to advantage in this 15 July 1961 scene as '4575' Class 2-6-2T No 5532 takes water after arrival with an evening 'auto-train' from Plymouth. It can be seen how the line falls away from the station towards Moorswater Viaduct, and also that the up platform did not extend as far westwards as the down side, thus allowing access to the yard. *Peter Gray*

As can be seen, the closure and subsequent lifting of the yard has allowed for the extension of the up platform. On 15 October 1992 an HST (power cars Nos 43090 and 43079) arrives with the 9.25 Penzance-Edinburgh. Liskeard still has a manual signalbox and its semaphore signals are now the first that a train will encounter on the journey westwards from Paddington.

LISKEARD (3): The Liskeard & Looe Railway branch platform was set at right-angles to the main line, and officially opened on 15 May 1901 after completion of a 2-mile connecting loop line to Coombe Junction; this sharply graded line negotiates a horseshoe curve *en route*. The platform has twice been extended, in 1924 and 1937, and is illustrated on 25 August 1960 as '4575' Class 2-6-2T No 5570 runs round after arriving with the 3.45pm from Looe. The connecting spur between the main and branch lines runs to the right of this scene. *Ron Lumber*

Trains still ply their way over this tortuous route, and on 13 October 1992 Gloucester RC&W Class '122' single-unit 'Bubble Car' No 122100 departs with the 12.00 service to Looe. The area to the right is now occupied by a car park. Poor road access to Looe has ensured the line's survival and patronage of the train service is encouraged by these 'park and ride' facilities.

COOMBE JUNCTION (1) is the location where the 1901 extension joined the original 1860 route of the Liskeard & Looe Railway. This latter line was built to replace the 6-mile Liskeard & Looe Union Canal which ran from Moorswater to Terras Pill, south of Sandplace, where it joined the Looe River.

Trains to Looe have to reverse at Coombe Junction before continuing their journey. On 9 July 1961 'Prairie' tank No 4574 has arrived from Liskeard with a short goods train. The signal box is clearly visible on the left whilst the passenger halt is located beyond the signal on the right. Moorswater Viaduct dominates the view in the background. *R. C. Riley*

The signal box was closed in 1981 and demolished. The track past the halt has been singled and the junction is now controlled by a ground frame. The current scene is pictured on 13 October 1992.

COOMBE JUNCTION (2): The second view of this location was taken at 9.05 am on 2 August 1958 from the overbridge just visible in the background of the previous scene, and illustrates a hive of activity with '4575' Class 2-6-2T No 4585 standing at the platform, having just arrived with the 8.40 from Looe, while on the right an unidentified sister engine is leaving from the loop with the 8.45 Liskeard-Looe. The halt opened with the loop to Liskeard, and replaced a station at Moorswater which closed from 15 May 1901.
Peter Gray

Today's simplified layout is pictured on 5 April 1992. The line north from here survives for a short way to serve the clay dries at Moorswater. However, here we see the annual visit of the Chipman's weedkilling train, which since 1989 has been operated by Class '20' locomotives sold by BR to Hunslet-Barclay. This working had left Laira at 9.00 for a visit to the Gunnislake branch and, after returning to Plymouth and a journey down the Cornish main line, it is now heading for Moorswater before tackling the Looe branch. The shunter has unlocked the No 2 Ground Frame to allow No 20904 forward. The train is tailed by No 20901.

21

MOORSWATER SHED: The Liskeard & Caradon Railway opened in two stages, the northern section in 1844 and the remainder in 1846. Originally worked by horses, steam locomotion was introduced in 1861. The railway was built to serve a mining district, with copper ore and granite being the main products. There was also a healthy inwards traffic in coal. At Moorswater the railway connected initially with the Liskeard & Looe Union Canal and then subsequently with the Liskeard & Looe Railway. Its two-road engine shed is believed to date from 1863 and was enlarged in 1878. The site also included machine and blacksmith's shops and a carriage repair building. The LCR closed on 1 January 1917 but its engine shed was to survive for a further 40 years or so as a sub-shed to

St Blazey. It is pictured here on 2 September 1961 with '4575' Class No 5573 resting outside. The truncated remains of the Caradon line run to the right of the building. *Peter Gray*

By 13 September 1992 a haulage company was occupying the site as part of an industrial estate. The existing track to the clay works is not far to the left of this scene.

CAUSELAND: Passenger services over the Liskeard & Looe Railway did not commence until 11 September 1879 when three stations were opened at Moorswater, Causeland and Looe. The original intermediate stop is situated in a quiet, picturesque and underpopulated location with no obvious reason for its existence. On 8 July 1960 '4500' Class No 4569 was captured for posterity as it arrived at the halt with a Liskeard to Looe train; at least two travellers will be joining for the journey southwards. This engine class was introduced to the line during the 1920s and continued to provide the motive power until services were dieselised from 11 September 1961. *Hugh Davies*

The station survives today as a request stop. Its flower beds have been created by the owners of adjacent holiday homes.

SANDPLACE station opened in 1881, located just north of a basin where the canal terminated after the railway wa[s] built. Nearby was a loop siding which closed in 1951 and was removed five years later. The station itself was buil[t] as a short single platform with a basic shelter. On 8 July 1958 Class '4575' 2-6-2T No 5557 arrives with the 2.00 p[m] Looe-Liskeard. *Terry Gough*

Thirty-four years on the scene is little changed other than the train. On 15 October 1992 Class '122' 'Bubbl[e] Cars' Nos 122100 and 122112 depart with the 9.45 Liskeard-Looe, having picked up a solitary passenger.

LOOE (1): The town comprises two communities on either side of the estuary of the River Looe and linked by a 19th-century bridge of seven low arches. Historically a fishing port, the harbour also provided an outlet for the mines and quarries in the Caradon area and this led to the building of the Liskeard & Looe Railway. The line terminated at the quayside in East Looe, the more important of the twin towns. Passenger services commenced in 1879 but were not fully developed until the opening of the extension to Liskeard. Looe station was located north of the harbour area and is pictured on 29 July 1958 as '4575' Class 2-6-2T No 4585 takes water. *Peter Gray*

Rationalisation of the station area occurred on 28 April 1968 when the track was truncated and the platform shortened at the south end. On 13 October 1992 Class '122' single unit No 122100 (55000) is seen just before its 12.28 departure to Liskeard.

LOOE (2): The southern end of the station is illustrated on 29 July 1958, with 'Prairie' tank No 4585 having arrive with the 2.52 pm from Liskeard. The track in the foreground continued to a small goods yard and a run-roun loop for passenger trains. At one time there were also small carriage and engine sheds, the latter closing in 191 Beyond the goods yard the rails continued to Buller Quay; this section was removed in 1954. Although still working port, greater prosperity for Looe lay in its development as a holiday resort. As a result of this, in th 1930s the GWR planned to build a more direct route to the town, and some preliminary work was undertake before the scheme was aborted with the advent of the Second World War. *Peter Gray*

Goods traffic ended in Novembe 1963 and the yard was lifted in th following year. Initially the orig nal platform and its single trac were retained, but these were su stantially shortened in 196 Subsequently a car park covere much of the site but more recentl another station has been built, th time occupied by the local consta ulary! In the 1992 scene the rai can just be seen beyond and to th left of the main building.

DOUBLEBOIS: Back on the main line again, this station, opened on 1 June 1860, served both a hamlet of the same name and the larger town of Dobwalls a little to the east. The west end is seen here on 2 August 1958 as Collett 'Grange' 4-6-0 No 6855 *Saighton Grange* and Churchward '4300' 2-6-0 No 5336 pass with the 8.15 am Perranporth-Paddington summer Saturday working. A goods yard was located on the down side just to the other side of the road overbridge, and the line descended from here for nearly 6 miles to Bodmin Road. War Department sidings were installed at the east end during the Second World War, and these were subsequently occupied as a permanent way depot. *Peter Gray*

The author can recall catching an auto-train to Plymouth from here in the early 1960s when a diesel shunter was stabled in a siding behind the down platform. However, all was soon to change as the station closed from 5 October 1964 and all of the connections to the sidings were taken out of use in 1968. Today it is hard to believe that the station ever existed.

BODMIN ROAD (1): Although it was Cornwall's county town, Bodmin's geographical position meant that it w[as] bypassed when the Cornwall Railway opened. Instead, the town's residents had to make the 3-mile journey to t[he] station, built in an attractive setting in the densely wooded Glynn Valley. On 3 May 1964 it received an unusu[al] visitor in the shape of unrebuilt Bulleid 'Pacific' No 34002 *Salisbury*, working 'The Cornubian', a PRC/RCTS ra[il] tour from Exeter to Penzance which was to be the final steam run over the Cornish main line until the GW150 c[el] ebrations in 1985. The special had been worked as far as Plymouth by ex-GWR 2-8-0 No 2887. *Hugh Ballantyne*

Re-named Bodmin Parkway from 4 November 1983, the station has reverted to its original role since the closu[re] of the Bodmin branch. On a gloriously sunny 20 September 1992, the 10.20 Paddington-Penzance HST calls, wi[th] power cars Nos 43147 and 43182 at either end.

BODMIN ROAD (2): Several fruitless attempts were made to link Bodmin to the main line before finally on 27 May 1887 a 3 miles 43 chains branch was opened. Despite its short length, construction was difficult with the line continually climbing to its destination with gradients as severe as 1 in 37. The railway was built to standard gauge in anticipation of the eventual conversion of the broad gauge main line, and accordingly for five years there was no connection between them. For many years the ubiquitous '45xx' 'Prairie' tanks provided the motive power over the line, but by 14 July 1961 Type 2 diesel-hydraulics (later Class '22') had arrived on the scene. Here No D6317 waits departure from the branch platform with a Wadebridge train. *R. C. Riley*

Passenger services ceased from 30 January 1967 but china clay traffic from Wenford ensured the line's survival until 1983. Happily trains are now running over the branch again under the auspices of the Bodmin & Wenford Railway, the Duchy's first standard gauge preserved railway. During a successful Diesel Gala on 20 September 1992, Class '20' No D8110 stands with the 15.20 to Bodmin General. This preserved engine was on loan from the South Devon Railway. *Photo courtesy of the Bodmin & Wenford Railway*

BODMIN GENERAL: The delightful terminus is illustrated on 10 September 1960 as 2-6-2T No 4565 runs around the 11.35 am Padstow-Bodmin Road. Visible on the left is the stone-built single road engine shed, with the signal box at the end of the platform and the g de b l m t a right. Coming into V A A is als to rebuild the line to Wenford to reduce the level of road traffic from the clay dries. The preserved Bodmin & Wenford Railway has already made its mark by carrying a regular traffic of light fittings from Bodmin to an exchange siding at Bodmin Parkway, from where it was worked north by BR. Unfortunately this finished in December 1992 due to a number of reasons, not least of which was BR's Government-enforced pricing policies.

In the meantime it is again possible to see a steam locomotive running around its train. On 21 August 1992 it was 0-6-0ST *Swiftsure*. On the right is Class '50' No 50042 *Triumph* while preserved Class '08' No D3559 *Triumph* can be glimpsed in the background.

Rails across the border

BUDE (1): The Devon & Cornwall Railway reached Holsworthy in 1879, but it was to be over 19 years before the LSWR extended the line a further 10 miles and into the Duchy, with services commencing on 10 August 1898. A short branch was also constructed to link the railway with Bude's canal basin. The terminus is pictured here on September 1965 as Ivatt 2-6-2T No 41283 runs round a Great Western Society railtour; this was the last occasion that a steam engine worked over the line. Also visible are the 36-lever signal box and the single-road engine shed with water tank behind, whilst a DMU sits in the bay platform. *Ron Lumber*

Since closure the railway has been erased from the landscape and a housing estate developed on the site of the station. One of the access roads has been named Bulleid Way in remembrance of the previous occupation.

BUDE (2): At 12.22 pm on 2 July 1966 a DMU arrives in the main platform with the 11.25 am from Okehampton. Bude's railway days are numbered and the final trains will run three months later on 1 October. The goods shed can be seen on the left, but freight services had already been withdrawn from 7 September 1964. Goods traffic over the branch was never particularly heavy and largely depended on agricultural produce. The gas works can be seen in the distance behind the engine shed; this had been enlarged in the 1950s and was supplied by coal brought in by both rail and sea. The wharf branch trailed away to the right between the gas works and signal box. *John Lumber*

In October 1992 a gasometer marks the site of the works, and part of the cutting on the approach to the station survives. A footpath follows the route of the wharf line.

CALSTOCK VIADUCT: The Plymouth, Devonport & South Western Junction Railway constructed an impressi
viaduct to provide a crossing of the River Tamar. It is built of concrete blocks and has 12 arches, each of 60-fo
span. A wagon lift was also erected adjacent to the viaduct to provide access to Calstock Quay below, but this w
closed in September 1934 and dismantled the following month. Easing over the viaduct on 4 August 1960 is '0
Class 0-4-4T No 30225 with the 5.23 pm Bere Alston to Callington. Fortunately the survival of this branch as far
Gunnislake means that it is still possible to enjoy the fine views from this imposing 290-yard-long structure. *Hu
Ballantyne*

CALSTOCK station is situated on a sharp right-angled curve at the end of the viaduct. It has only ever had one pla
form, but once possessed a small goods yard, including one siding that led to the wagon lift. Colonel H.
Stephens, the well-known operator of light railways, was appointed Associate Engineer to the PD&SWJR and h
hand was detectable in the station buildings, which were to a simple design of corrugated iron constructio
Pausing at the station on 4 July 1961 is Ivatt 2-6-2T No 41317 heading the 4.23 pm Callington to Bere Alston. *Ter
Gough*

The sidings were taken out of use on 4 August 1966 and the passing loop suffered similarly on 5 May 1968. Th
former goods yard has now been fenced off and housing recently erected on part of the site. On 15 October 19
Metro-Cammell DMU No 101680 was working the 14.35 Gunnislake-Plymouth.

GUNNISLAKE (1): Much of the Callington branch had its origins in the 3ft 6ins gauge East Cornwall Mineral
Railway. There had been intense mining activity in the area during the 19th century and improved transportation
was needed to bring in the coal required by the mines and ship out the ore to Calstock Quay. Various plans for
railway culminated in the ECMR, which was officially opened throughout on 8 May 1872. The line was highly successful and it was soon considered desirable that it be connected to the main railway system. Again there were

several schemes before agreemen
was reached for the PD&SWJR to
purchase the undertaking and con
nect it to its main line from
Lydford to Devonport at Ber
Alston, a route that was leased to
the LSWR. The branch was const
tuted as a separate company, the
Bere Alston & Calstock Ligh
Railway, and opened on 2 March
1908. It was built to standard gaug
and joined the erstwhile ECMR at
point just south of Gunnislake. O
1 April 1961 '02' No 30225 i
depicted leaving the station with
the 1.00 pm Callington-Bere Alston
The other side of the island pla
form is occupied by No 41317 on
through Plymouth to Callington
working. *Peter Gray*

The same view today is large
obscured by foliage, but the pla
form and its simple shelter can b
noted in the distance.

GUNNISLAKE (2): The station was built on the site of the ECMR's Drakewalls depot, with access to the island platform being via a short subway under the down line. The station can be seen to advantage in this 4 July 1961 view. The signal box was just to the left of this scene. *Terry Gough*

The up siding and the two down sidings in the immediate foreground were taken out of use on 2 August 1966, goods traffic on the branch having officially ceased earlier in the year. The down loop and adjacent siding were disconnected on 5 May 1968. Only the former up track now remains, but finishes just to the left of the present-day photo. The line beyond here was officially closed from 7 November 1966, with the track being removed in the following year. The survival of the branch to this point is due to it serving a geographically remote area which has poor road access to Plymouth.

The third view, taken on 15 October 1992 and from a position to the right of the last scene, shows Regional Railways-liveried Class '101' No 101680 arriving with the 13.45 from Plymouth. Four passengers are waiting to make the return journey.

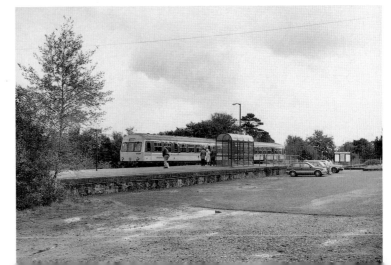

CHILSWORTHY HALT was opened on 1 June 1909, its position allowing passengers a superb view across the Tamar Valley, as can be appreciated from this 4 July 1961 photograph. In 1914 a siding was laid behind the photographer's position to serve a brickworks, the products of which were shipped from Calstock Quay. To the right of this view another siding once led to the Clitters Mine. *Terry Gough*

The access path from the road now forms part of a public footpath, but the trackbed is heavily overgrown. Only a little 'gardening' has allowed this view of the far end of the halt and the road overbridge.

LATCHLEY was another small halt, located about a mile from Chilsworthy. It had a simple corrugated iron shelter on the platform, and until its removal some time before this 12 July 1955 photo, it also boasted a siding on the up side which ran in front of the station house and adjacent to the loading platform of the former ECMR's Cox's Park Depot. The ungated road leads to the village of Latchley, about a mile away. *R. C. Riley*

The scene in October 1992 shows the station house, which is still used as a residence, and the platform which unfortunately will never see a train again.

LUCKETT station was named Stoke Climsland on the opening of the line, but following complaints that this village was some distance away, it was renamed from 1 November 1909. It had a single platform and a passing loop, next to which was a loading bank, a remnant of the mineral railway's public depot known as Monks Corner. On 4 July 1961 'Prairie' tank No 41317 stands at the platform on a Callington to Bere Alston train. The Ivatt tanks had first appeared on the line a few years earlier when they displaced two Hawthorn Leslie 0-6-0Ts which had worked the route from 1907. Initially they shared duties with the Adams '02' 0-4-4Ts which had operated on the branch from 1929, but the LMS engines dominated the line in the last few years until dieselisation in 1964. *Terry Gough*

The original ECMR station house is now occupied privately, and is illustrated together with the grass-covered platform.

CALLINGTON: From Luckett to the terminus the line ran along the edges of Kit Hill and some three-quarters of a mile beyond the former station were Kit Hill Sidings. From these a narrow gauge tramway ran up to quarries on the hillside. Somewhat typically the end of the branch was actually in Kelly Bray, about a mile north of Callington, and the ECMR depot had carried that name. The station is pictured on 7 July 1958 as '02' No 30192 runs around after arriving with the 3.15 pm from Bere Alston; it was necessary to back a train out of the platform to complete this manoeuvre. Just visible on the left is the timber-built two-road engine shed, a sub-shed to Plymouth Friary. Behind the photographer was an overall roof which covered the platform and adjacent track. *Ron Lumber*

The last train from Callington departed at 7.40 pm on Saturday 5 November 1966. Today much of the site is an industrial estate, ironically named Beeching Park! However, Kit Hill still forms a backdrop to the present-day scene.

LAUNCESTON NORTH was the terminus of the Launceston & South Devon Railway, a broad gauge line built as an extension to the South Devon's Tavistock branch and which received its first train on 1 June 1865. Launceston is an ancient market town at the centre of a large agricultural district, but its importance had diminished during the first half of the 19th century, not least due to the delayed arrival of the railway. This station remained independent of the later LSWR route until 1943 when a connecting line was installed as an emergency measure during the Second World War. The suffix 'North' was added to the name in 1951, but the station closed to passengers on 30 June of the following year, when traffic was diverted over the connection to the Southern station. It remained in use as a goods depot, but on the closure of the branch, from 31 December 1962, supervision passed to the Southern Region. On 5 September 1965 it was visited by a steam engine for the last time when 2-6-2T No 41283 hauled a Great Western Society special marking the centenary of the railway reaching the town. *Ron Lumber*

The goods depot finally closed on 28 February 1966 and the site now forms part of an industrial estate. The background buildings serve as reference points when comparing the two scenes.

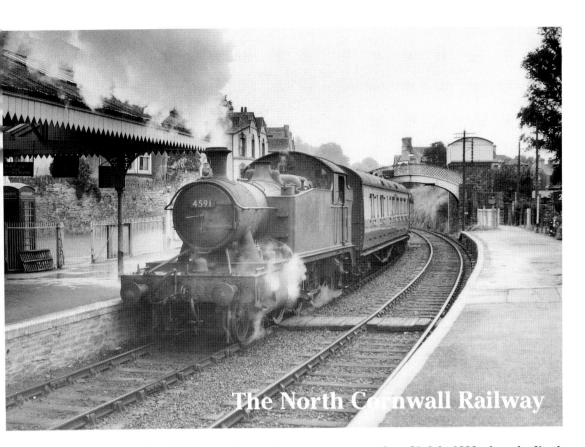

The North Cornwall Railway

LAUNCESTON SOUTH (1): The LSWR's services to the town commenced on 21 July 1886 when the North Cornwall's route from Halwill was opened. Its single track crossed the River Tamar via a girder bridge, and then also crossed the GWR branch before the two routes entered the town and their adjacent, parallel stations. From 1952 both routes used the Southern station and on 1 July 1959 ex-GWR 2-6-2T No 4591 is pictured in the down platform with a branch train for Plymouth. *Rodney Lissenden*

The last services over the branch ran on 29 December 1962 when the final train for Plymouth should have departed at 8.35 pm. However, the previous departure (the 5.40) had encountered heavy delays caused by deteriorating weather conditions and eventually arrived 3 hours late in Plymouth. Meanwhile, the 6.20 pm Plymouth-Launceston was also badly affected by the heavy snowfalls, reaching Tavistock South over 5 hours late at 12.25 am on the next day. It was unable to proceed any further and accordingly Launceston was not to be served by what should have been its final trains over the branch.

The present view of the station site shows that it is now occupied as a car park by the Launceston Steam Railway, the station for which is located just on the other side of the road overbridge visible in the distance.

LAUNCESTON SOUTH (2): The west end of the station is seen at 3.45 pm on 11 July 1964 as 'N' Class 2-6-0 No 31859 calls with the 10.35 Waterloo-Padstow. The signalman is walking along the up platform with the single-line tablet which he will hand to the footplate crew. The picturesque signal box is clearly visible, whilst the track behind it forms part of the erstwhile GWR station. Out of the picture on the right is the goods yard, which once handled a substantial volume of cattle traffic, and a turntable and single-road engine shed were also located here. *Ron Lumber*

Goods services over the North Cornwall line ceased from 7 September 1964, with total closure of the line from Wadebridge on 3 October 1966. Today only the semaphore signal on the right hints at the railway activity once to be seen here.

The Launceston Steam Railway is now based just to the west of the former South station, and its 2-foot gauge track runs for a couple of miles over the former North Cornwall route. Its station is seen here (*above*) on 20 August 1992 just after the saddle tank *Lilian* had arrived with its train. In the foreground is *Covertcoat*, another of the line's engines.

EGLOSKERRY: Extension of the North Cornwall Railway was exceedingly slow, due to a combination of insufficient finance and difficult terrain, and it was to be a further six years before the railway was opened to Tresmeer. From Launceston the rails followed the Kensey Valley and after some 4 miles of gentle climbing they reached the village of Egloskerry. The station is pictured at 2.12 pm on a sunny 11 July 1964 with 'N' 2-6-0 No 31855 awaiting departure with the 1.00 pm Padstow-Okehampton; the engine later worked back on the 5.51 Okehampton-Wadebridge. In addition to a passing loop, the station also had a small goods yard which was located to the right behind the signal box. *Ron Lumber*

The brick-built station building is now occupied as a dwelling, with bed and breakfast facilities on offer. The platforms are buried in the verdant garden, but careful study of the August 1992 scene reveals the station nameboard between the two bushes on the left. Workshops now occupy the site of the goods yard.

TRESMEER: This was the next station on the line, opening on 28 July 1892, a month behind schedule due to a landslip. To reach this point the route's gradients had become more severe as the line headed towards the high plateau which forms Cornwall's backbone. Egloskerry and Tresmeer stations are immortalised in a verse of Sir John Betjeman, and certainly their very Cornish names have a poetic ring to them. One wonders what the former poet Laureate would have done if Tresmeer had been named after the hamlet of Splatt where the station was actually located! The main building was also constructed of brick, but from hereon the line's stations were more typically built of local stone. Tresmeer was photographed from the adjacent roadbridge at around 5.00 pm on 22 August 1964. The signal box, which was located on the up platform, closed on 14 November 1965 when both the up line and goods yard were taken out of use. *Peter Gray*

The station is now a private residence with the platforms incorporated in the garden.

OTTERHAM station was located about a mile from the line's summit, some 800 feet above sea level. The landscape here is flat and open and affords a distant glimpse of the Atlantic Ocean. This view was taken on 3 September 1966, a month before closure, and shows two single-car units forming the 4.50 pm Okehampton-Wadebridge service. The North Cornwall Railway was single track throughout but each of the intermediate stations had crossing loops controlled by signal boxes. The track in the down loop here had been taken out of use on 7 February 196 and was removed the following October. *Ron Lumber*

The 'past' photograph was taken from an overbridge, but this has been demolished since the line closed, and the road widened. The area between the platforms has been filled in, but the edging slabs of the former up platform are clearly identifiable in the August 1992 scene. The building has been used as a house but was unoccupied at the time of this visit. The rest of the site is now part of a caravan park.

AMELFORD station opened on 14 August 1893 when the railway was extended from Tresmeer, and is pictured ere at around 4.00 pm on 29 August 1960 as 'N' Class 2-6-0 No 31836 pauses with a down goods train, waiting to ross an up passenger service. This area of the Duchy is full of the myth of King Arthur; for a long time the small wn of Camelford was synonymous with Camelot, whilst Tintagel, some 5 miles distant, was reputedly Arthur's irthplace. Legend tells us that he received his mortal wound at Slaughter Bridge and it is historical fact that this as the site of a battle where the Celtic Cornish were defeated by the Saxons. Camelford station was located near ae site of the battlefield and just a mile or so from the town. *Ron Lumber*

Today the station is occupied by the Museum of Historic Cycling, with an extension added to the main building increase the exhibition space. A visit is recommended, not only to view the contents but also the many features f the station that have been preserved. The current owner removed the platform canopy as it had become badly ecayed, but the stanchions have been restored in situ. Just visible on the right of the present scene is the derelict oods shed which is under different ownership.

DELABOLE: The winding 2$\frac{1}{2}$-mile long Camelford to Delabole section of the NCR opened on 18 October 18? During its course the railway afforded a good view of Cornwall's highest hills, Brown Willy (1,375 feet) and Rou Tor, before beginning its descent towards sea level. On the approach to Delabole the line passed close to t ancient slate quarry, reputed to be the biggest man-made excavation in Europe. The quarry company was pleased at the coming of the railway that three-quarters of a mile of trackbed was provided free of char Delabole station is seen on 19 September 1964 while Standard Class '3MT' 2-6-2T No 82030 waits with an up p senger train. The down platform is occupied by the 9.50 am from Okehampton. *Ron Lumber*

The station building is now dwelling, and the up platform h been excavated. When the site w visited in August 1992 a sm housing estate known as 'T Sidings' was being developed ov the trackbed in the background.

KEW HIGHWAY (1): Shortly
er Port Isaac Road station the
R passed through its only tun-
l, a 333-yard curved bore named
elill after a nearby village. The
xt station was sited adjacent to
e main Camelford to Wadebridge
ad, approximately 1¹/₂ miles
m the village of St Kew. The
in buildings were located on the
side and are pictured on 12 July
61. As with the other intermedi-
e stations between Launceston
d Wadebridge there was no foot-
idge, and passengers had to use
boarded crossing to gain access
the down platform. *R. C. Riley*
The station building survives as a
sidence with the space between
e platforms filled in, but a differ-
t form of transport dominates
is 20 August 1992 view.
The third photograph shows a
sy scene on 27 April 1963 as pre-
rved 'T9' 4-4-0 No 120 stands in
e down platform whilst working
RCTS/PRC railtour from Exeter.
e participants are taking the
portunity to explore the station
ilst waiting to cross an up train.
e signal box is visible on the left;
is closed on 21 November 1965
en the track through the station
s singled. *Ron Lumber*

ST KEW HIGHWAY (2): Another view from 27 April 1963 shows the two classes of engine most closely associa[ted] with the North Cornwall line. Dugald Drummond's graceful 'T9' 4-4-0s worked the route for many years until 19[ ] when the surviving examples were withdrawn from Exmouth Junction shed. No 30120 was one of these, but it w[as] claimed for the National Collection, given an overhaul at Eastleigh Works, painted in LSWR livery and subseque[nt]-ly assigned to special duties. Here the railtour has been held to cross the 12.58 Padstow-Okehampton which [is] arriving behind Maunsell 'N' Cl[ass] 2-6-0 No 31874. The SECR 'Mogu[l] first appeared in the West in 19[ ] and capably carried out th[ese] duties for 40 years, until virtua[lly] the end of steam working in [the] area. *Ron Lumber*

Today it is difficult to imag[ine] that the railway ever existed he[re]. However, the faint indentation [in] the foreground grass in the Aug[ust] 1992 view marks the edge of [the] former up platform.

ADEBRIDGE (1): Services to this station over the NCR commenced on 1 June 1895, but the town had already had ailway for over 60 years, the Bodmin & Wadebridge Railway having opened on 4 July 1834. This pioneer line s the first in Cornwall to use steam power and had been conceived primarily to carry sea-sand inland from adebridge for use as manure. The two railways originally converged at Wadebridge Junction, but from July 07 the connection was removed and the signal box closed. The two routes then entered Wadebridge on parallel cks, giving the appearance of a double-track railway. An island platform was added to the station when it was larged to accommodate the NCR. On 22 July 1960 'T9' 4-4-0 No 30313 is pictured leaving this platform with a rth Cornwall line service. The roof of the canopy for the coal stage can be noted to the right of the engine, hind which was located the two-road engine shed. *R. C. Riley*

The North Cornwall line closed m 3 October 1966, with passen- r services to Bodmin ending m 30 January 1967; the track yout was rationalised later that ar to cater for the remaining ight traffic. Since final closure a using estate has been developed much of the station site, but the ne-built goods shed survives as arts centre, seen on the left of is 20 August 1992 photograph.

WADEBRIDGE (2): 'Greyhound' 4-4-0 No 30717 stands in the down platform with a Padstow train on 30 June 19[...] This platform and the main station buildings were constructed in 1888 when the B&WR was connected to [...] GWR's Bodmin branch. There was some irony in this development as the B&WR had been owned by the latte[...] great rivals, the LSWR, for over 40 years. At the time of purchase the nearest point served by the LSWR was s[...] some 120 miles away, but the move was designed solely to keep the broad gauge out of North Cornwall. *Rod[...] Lissenden*

In its last days the freight traffic from Wadebridge mainly comprised crushed slate from Delabole, but t[...] ceased towards the end of 1977 when the quarry company went into liquidation. Other commodities carr[...] included cement and fertiliser, [...] the booked daily trip rarely ran [...] 1978, and it is believed that [...] final freight operated in August [...] that year. A railtour from the E[...] Midlands ran on 30 Septemb[...] with the final trains running on [...] December when the Bodmin Li[...] Club operated two DMU 'San[...] Specials' from Bodmin Road. T[...] main station building has n[...] been converted and extended [...] form the 'John Betjeman Centre [...] the Retired'. You can now dri[...] your car along 'Southern Wa[...] which has been constructed ov[...] part of the track formation.

TLE PETHERICK CREEK: The North Cornwall Railway was extended by some 5¹/₂ miles from Wadebridge to dstow with services commencing on 27 March 1899. This provided a most attractive journey, with the route run- g alongside the southern shore of the steadily broadening estuary of the River Camel. The rails had to cross vari- s side-creeks, and at Little Petherick Creek a curving iron bridge consisting of three 150-foot trusses was provid- . 'Battle of Britain' Class 4-6-2 No 34110 *66 Squadron* crosses the bridge on 3 July 1961 with the down 'Atlantic ast Express'. Only these lighter unrebuilt Bulleid 'Pacifics' were allowed to cross this structure. *Terry Gough* Today this stretch of line forms part of the Camel Trail, a public footpath which enables walkers to sample the lendid views once enjoyed by railway passengers. The bridge is pictured as the sun sets on 15 October 1992.

PADSTOW (1): Drummond Class 'T9' 4-4-0 No 30712 nears its destination with a local train in August 1957. Litt
Petherick Creek Bridge can be noted just above the locomotive, while Dennis Hill complete with its obelisk dom
nates the right background. The engine was built by Dubs & Co in June 1899 at a cost of £3,200, and was to l
withdrawn in November 1958 — good investment by anyone's sta
dards! *John Stredwick*

Thirty-five years on to tl
month, the present photograp
shows that the Camel Trail footpa
now follows the former trackbe
On a clear sunny day (a rare occu
rence in the summer of 1992!) tl
fishing vessel *Silvercloud* unde
goes repair.

PADSTOW (2): It had taken 17 years from authorisation for the railway to reach Padstow, a town that had suffered economic decline following the ending of its traditional shipbuilding industry. However, the arrival of the NCR prompted greater prosperity through fishing and tourism. The station is pictured during the evening of 27 April 1963 as preserved 'T9' No 120 waits before returning to Exeter with the RCTS/PRC special encountered earlier in this book. Prominent in the right background is the Hotel Metropole which opened in 1900, a year after the railway arrived. To the right was the fish market, built by the Harbour Authority and served by several sidings. *Ron Lumber* Goods services ended from 7 September 1964, whilst the last passenger trains ran on 28 January 1967. Today the main station building is occupied as offices, with a small snack bar standing on the truncated remains of the platform. Most of the site is now used as a car park.

Bodmin & Wadebridge Railway

GROGLEY HALT: As part of a number of improvements to the B&WR in 1888, a deviation was made to the origi[nal] route near Grogley to avoid a sharp curve. Part of the original formation was, however, retained as a headshunt [to] gain access to the 1-mile-long Ruthern Bridge branch. This freight-only line received its first train on 6 Aug[ust] 1834, with the final one running [on] 29 November 1933. It was built [to] serve local tin and iron mines, [but] after their closure it only carri[ed] sporadic agricultural traff[ic]. Grogley Halt was located close [to] the junction with the branch, a[nd] on 10 September 1960 we see Cla[ss] '02' 0-4-4T No 30200 about hal[f a] mile from its single platform wi[th] the 4.05 pm Bodmin Nort[h-] Padstow. This attractive class too[k] over the local passenger services [in] the 1920s and remained on tho[se] duties until 1961. *Peter Gray*

The same view today is alm[ost] totally obscured by undergrow[th]. The light patch just discernible [in] the left foreground is the Cam[el] Trail footpath.

NANSTALLON HALT: Steam railmotors were intoduced on B&WR passenger turns on 1 June 1906. Subsequently, [on] 2 July, three halts were opened at Grogley, Nanstallon and Dunmere. The second of these is pictured here, [lo]oking eastwards in 1962. Although an LSWR station, it is interesting to note that the waiting hut is of the 'pago-[da]' style more commonly associated with the GWR. A level crossing controlled by a signal box was located behind [th]e photographer. A little further westwards was a siding which had closed from 2 May 1960. *Lens of Sutton*
[?]The platform is still in situ alongside the footpath, but is partly obscured in this 7 February 1993 view by the [wo]oden fencing.

BOSCARNE JUNCTION (1): Ex-GWR 2-6-2T No 4565 passes the signal box on 9 August 1960 with a Wadebridge
Bodmin Road train, taking the line to Bodmin General which was opened on 3 September 1888. The signal box
marked the end of the single-line section from Wadebridge East and also controlled an adjacent level crossing.
Rodney Lissenden

The line from here to Bodmin General is now owned, but not yet operated, by the preserved Bodmin &
Wenford Railway and the present view, taken on 21 August 1992, shows wagons belonging to this company -
the foreground are two clayhoods. The track beyond this point was lifted following closure to Wadebridge, so the
wagons mark the current extent of the railway, on rails that are still in situ due to the continuation of Wenford
trains until 1983, although one siding has been removed to accommodate the Camel Trail on the other side of the
wooden fence to the right.

BOSCARNE JUNCTION (2): The eastern end of the site is illustrated on 19 September 1964 as it is explored by participants of the Plymouth Railway Circle's brake-van tour on its return from Wenford. The train is headed by ex-GWR 0-6-0PT No 1369, whilst on the right a diesel railbus stands at Boscarne Exchange Platform. A pair of plat-

forms were constructed in May 1964 at a cost of £2,000, and from 15 June passengers who were conveyed by railbus from Bodmin North could transfer to Bodmin Road-Wadebridge services at this point. A rail-level platform was built for the former line, while a normal height platform was provided on the other route. In this view the railbus is unusually positioned at the latter to allow a path for the railtour. *Peter Gray*

The weed-choked trackwork presents a forlorn sight on 20 August 1992. Hopefully a happier scene will be visible in the not to distant future if the projected rejuvenation of the Wenford clay traffic materialises.

DUNMERE JUNCTION on 19 September 1964, with pannier tank No 1369 on the PRC tour. This engine was one of three which had been displaced from their previous duties on the Weymouth Quay branch, being transferred to Wadebridge shed in 1962 to replace the veteran Beattie tanks. The train is on the original B&WR main line to Wenfordbridge which opened on 30 September 1834, while the rails in the foreground form the branch to Bodmin North. Prior to 1895 the junction was a little to the south of this spot, but a deviation was constructed to eliminate a level crossing and to ease gradients. *Ron Lumber*

Bodmin North lost its railway service from 30 January 1967, while the Wenford line officially closed from 21 November 1983. At present both routes form part of the Camel Trail footpath and were being well used by walkers at the time of the author's visits in August 1992.

DUNMERE HALT was opened on 2 July 1906 and comparison with the photograph of Nanstallon Halt will show how similar they were. Neither was manned and tickets were issued and collected by the train guard. This 3 July 1961 view is looking towards Bodmin. The bridge in the background carries the main road from Bodmin to Wadebridge, and a short distance down this road is Dunmere level crossing (see page 65). *Terry Gough*

The 16 October 1992 scene shows that once again the platform still survives alongside the Camel Trail.

The third picture dates from 19 June 1956 and shows '02' Class No 30200 approaching the halt, and a gallery of camera-toting enthusiasts, with a two-coach train for Bodmin North. *Hugh Davies*

BODMIN NORTH: The original B&WR station at Bodmin was to prove inadequate, and during the reconstruction of the railway from 1886 the passenger service was suspended while a new station was built, which finally opened in 1895 after a gap of nine years. The main station building was single storey and of stone construction, and is seen here in August 1960 as ex-GWR 0-6-0PT No 4666 runs around its train before forming the 5.40 pm departure to Wadebridge. Two pannier tanks were allocated to Wadebridge shed early in 1960 and largely replaced the Adams '02s' from their long-standing duties. However, they were only to remain for some two years before being superceded by Ivatt 2-6-2Ts. *Ron Lumber*

After closure the site was cleared and the 20 September 1992 scene shows that a road runs along the former trackbed. The background buildings in the past view, including the former gaol in the far distance, are the best reference points when comparing the two views.

DUNMERE CROSSING was one of the features of the Wenfordbridge line, where the single-track railway passed over the main Bodmin to Wadebridge road by means of an ungated level crossing. This anachronistic working practice continued until the end of traffic over the branch, as can be seen in this 26 September 1983 photograph, which depicts the very last train of china clay from Wenford waiting to proceed behind Class '08' diesel shunter No 08113. The guard and travelling shunter are about to hold up the road traffic to allow the passage of the train. By this time the trip was booked to run thrice weekly, but the dwindling traffic meant that it actually operated less often. At one time there was a siding to the left of the train, but this was removed in 1969.
David Mitchell

Today the rails are still embedded in the road surface, but the area beyond the crossing now forms a car park for those wishing to use the Camel Trail.

WENFORD: China clay traffic commenced over the Bodmin & Wadebridge Railway in 1862 and eventually was to become the sole reason for the line's survival. The clay is mined on Stannon Moor, some 6 miles away, and is then pumped by pipeline to the dries at Wenford. It was originally taken by rail to the wharves at Wadebridge and Padstow, but after the GWR connected with the B&WR most was taken out by that route for export via the docks at Fowey. Here Beattie tank No 30587 is pictured alongside the clay works on 9 August 1960, having just arrived with a train of empties. *Rodney Lissenden*

The Stannon clay dries are still open, but all the china clay is presently taken away by lorry. However, the local road system is narrow and unsuited to this traffic, and at the time of writing there are proposals for the reinstatement of the railway.

WENFORDBRIDGE: The terminus of the B&WR was located nearly half-a-mile beyond the clay dries. The track layout at this depot was modified in 1926 when a 5-ton overhead crane was installed. The 'past' photograph was taken from this crane and shows 0-6-0PT No 1369 after it has arrived with the RCTS/PRC 'Camel Valleyman' brakevan tour of 27 April 1963. One of the sidings here continued over an adjacent road and connected with a tramway to De Lank Quarries, a standard gauge line that ran up the hillside by means of a cable incline to the granite quarries. Traffic over the tramway ceased during the Second World War. *Ron Lumber*

The Wenfordbridge goods depot closed from 13 February 1967 and the track was lifted from here to just north of Wenford clay works during 1971. Latterly the principal traffic had been coal, and although today the site is used as a coal yard, unfortunately fresh stocks now arrive by lorry. The crane has been removed and the present photo had to be taken from ground level. The hut visible in the past view is now decaying behind the tree on the right, while a small part of the fence next to where most of the railtourers are standing can be found beyond the coal-pile.

Lostwithiel to St Blazey

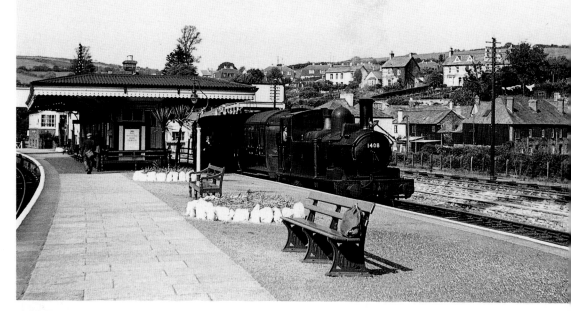

LOSTWITHIEL (1) is an ancient town which since the Middle Ages has served as a commercial and administrative centre for an area of mid-Cornwall. Its economy was boosted by the arrival of the Cornwall Railway, particularly as it elected to locate its main workshops here. Its importance as a railway centre was further enhanced when the Lostwithiel & Fowey Railway opened on 1 June 1869 to serve the jetties at Carne Point, just short of Fowey. However, the subsequent opening of the Cornwall Mineral Railway's line to Fowey had a disastrous effect on the branch's traffic and it was closed on 31 December 1879. Eventually, however, it was rebuilt to standard gauge, extended to join the CMR line and re-opened on 16 September 1895. This time a passenger service was operated in addition to freight, the passenger trains, for many years auto-trains, working from a bay platform. On 11 June 1956 '14xx' Class 0-4-2T No 1408 leaves with the 5.05 pm to Fowey. This was the only regular service to be operated by this class in the Duchy. *Michael Mensing*

With the withdrawal of passenger trains, the tracks adjacent to the bay platform now normally only see china clay wagons. However, they were devoid of traffic when photographed on 21 August 1992.

In the third photograph the east end of the station on 29 July 1958 provides a scene of activity. Collett 4-6-0 No 5972 *Olton Hall* is working the up 'Cornishman' while on the left 0-4-2T No 1419 is propelling auto-trailer No W168W forming an arrival from Fowey. *Peter Gray*

LOSTWITHIEL (2): On a wet and dismal 31 July 1981 Class '37' No 37203 returns with a train of china clay empties from Carne Point. The timber-bodied wagons were built in Swindon Works from about 1955, whilst the hooded covers were fitted from 1974 as a more effective method of protecting their valuable cargo. The original Cornwall Railway timber-built goods shed can be noted on the right of the photo. *David Mitchell*

Currently Lostwithiel is one of Cornwall's remaining pockets of semaphore signalling. On 21 August 1992 Class '122' 'Bubble Car' No 122100 is seen departing as the 16.40 Plymouth-Par. The goods shed was dismantled in 1982 and there were plans to re-erect it at a proposed preservation centre at Lanteague, near Shepherds. Unfortunately the failure of this project led to its destruction. A car park now occupies the site while the Cornwall Railway workshop buildings on the right are used as industrial units.

GOLANT: The Lostwithiel to Fowey branch follows the lovely valley of the River Fowey and hugs its west bank for much of the way. The only intermediate station served the village of Golant, opening on 1 July 1896. Passenger services over the line were subject to temporary closure during both World Wars, but finally succombed on 4 January 1965. *Lens of Sutton*

Happily the track survives as far as Carne Point for the conveyance of china clay to the docks. This picture of the site of the platform was taken on 7 February 1993. The sheds in the left background provide the best link when comparing the two scenes.

OWEY: The standard gauge Cornwall Mineral Railway opened on 1 June 1874, providing direct access from the eart of china clay country to the docks at Fowey, where the railway also constructed three large jetties south of arne Point. The St Blazey to Fowey section included Pinnock Tunnel which, at 1,173 yards, was the longest in ornwall. Passenger trains over this line commenced on 20 June 1876 but were poorly patronised and the service nly lasted until 8 July 1929. Those to Lostwithiel were to run for a good deal longer, however, and 0-4-2T No 1419 s seen on 25 August 1960 with the 1.45 pm departure. *Ron Lumber*

Fowey finally lost its passenger service on 4 January 1965. The route from Par to Fowey was sold to the English hina Clay Company in 1968, and it has now been converted to a private road for the Company's lorries. The railway now ends at Carne Point, about half a mile from this spot.

Our final view of this most picturesque line takes us back to Golant, where the railway crosses its harbour on a auseway. The line is seen to advantage from high above on 13 October 1992 as Class '37' No 37412 heads towards arne Point with a train of loaded CDA wagons. These air-braked wagons were introduced in 1988 to replace the acuum-braked wooden-bodied clay hoods. Golant Halt was located just to the right of this scene.

PAR (1) is dominated by its port and vast clay-drying plant. Opened in 1833, the former owes its existence
Joseph Treffry, a local landowner with interests in local mines and pits. He had been frustrated in his attempts
build a railway to Fowey Quay or obtain better rates from the owners of Charlestown Harbour, so the tidal ha
bour at Par was built as an alternative. The station opened with the Cornwall Railway on 4 May 1859, and here v
see the north end on 29 August 1959 as 2-6-2T No 5175 leaves the down loop with a goods train. *Peter Gray*

Par retains its signal box, and lower quadrant semaphore signals still control movements in the station area. C
12 October 1992 English Electric Class '37' No 37674 crosses from the down to the up main line before taking tl
Newquay branch with a train of clay empties from Carne Point to Goonbarrow Junction.

…AR (2) on 2 July 1960 as 0-6-0PT No 1664 pulls the Drinnick Mill goods towards St Blazey yard. The train has had …reverse after arriving behind another pannier tank, No 8733 of the '5700' Class, which is probably still at the …her end of the train. The large timber-built goods shed is visible in the background. The CMR opened a standard …uge loop from its own Par (later St Blazey) station to here on 1 January 1879, but there was to be no physical …nnection with the main line until the gauge conversion in 1892. *Peter Gray*

The goods shed was demolished and the sidings were altered for a new Freightliner Terminal, but this was …ortlived and only one siding survives for engineers' use. A track machine can be noted on 28 September 1992 as …37671 *Tre Pol and Pen* eases through the island platform with another Carne Point to Goonbarrow Junction …orking.

ST BLAZEY SHED: The CMR sited its headquarters at St Blazey with facilities including offices, workshops a[...] most notably, an unusual locomotive shed. Built in 1873 of red brick, the shed comprised a roundhouse with ni[...] roads leading to an external turntable. The original CMR locomotive stock consisted of 18 Sharp Stewart 0-6-0[...] designed to work back-to-back pairs, and each of the shed roa[...] was able to accommodate one pa[...] The depot's residents changed ov[...] the years, but the building was [...] remain in use for 113 years, mai[...] supplying small tank engines [...] power the china clay trains. On [...] July 1959 0-6-0PTs Nos 1624, 16[...] 7446 and 9655 are on display. [...] this time nearly 40 engines we[...] allocated here. *Terry Nicholls*

The shed closed to steam in Ap[...] 1962, but it continued to hou[...] diesels until final closure exac[...] 25 years later. The buildings, ho[...] ever, are listed, and following re[...] repairs and the construction [...] internal walls, the roundhouse [...] now occupied as industrial units[...]

Routes to Newquay

BLAZEY BRIDGE CROSSING: Another of Treffry's projects was the constuction of a canal some 2 miles long
king Ponts Mill with Par Harbour. Completed in 1835, the canal provided an outlet for the vast Fowey Consuls
ne at Tywardreath. In 1855 a horse-drawn tramway was built alongside the canal and this was reconstructed by
e CMR by 1 June 1874 when the through line from Fowey to Newquay was opened to goods. This crossing over
e A390 road is located on this stretch of railway. On 22 May 1959 one of the crew on the footplate of 2-6-2T No
74 is about to collect the single-line token whilst approaching the crossing with the 11.30 am Newquay-Par train.
signal box is just out of view to the left. *Michael Mensing*
The box closed in 1973 and the token apparatus has been removed. A garage now occupies the site to the right
d this 16 October 1992 view shows a more cluttered scene as Class '153' No 153318 approaches on the 9.30
wquay-Par. Another hut has been erected in front of the one visible in the past scene.
As a postscript it is worth noting that at one time all of this area was under the sea, but centuries of mining and
ting up have moved the shoreline southwards.

were the 947-yard-long, 1 in 10, rope-worked Carmears Incline, and a magnificent 10-arch, 216-yard-long granite viaduct/aqueduct. When the CMR was incorporated to operate and rebuild Treffry's tramways, a new line was built in the Luxulyan Valley avoiding the incline. The new route passed under the the graceful 98-foot-high viaduct which still stands as a monument to Treffry's enterprise. The past view shows 'Grange' 4-6-0 No 6812 *Chesford Grange* running into Luxulyan with the 12.25pm Par-Newquay on 8 July 1961. The siding on the right is on the alignment of the original tramway, which until 1933 still saw occasional traffic from Colcerrow Quarry. *Peter Gray*

The siding was taken out of use in 1964, and the same view today features Class '122' No 122112 as it passes by on 12 October 1992 with the 16.25 Newquay-Par.

79

LUXULYAN (2): 'Bridges for Luxulyan' station opened on 20 June 1876 when passenger services commenced over the Cornwall Mineral Railway's Fowey to Newquay line; it was re-named Luxulyan from 1 May 1905. Originally there were two platforms, but the station layout was revised in 1910 when an island platform was provided. The site is seen here to advantage on 13 July 1961 as pannier tank No 1664 heads for St Blazey with the Goonbarrow branch goods. The water tower, pagoda-style platform hut and signal box are all clearly visible. *Peter Gray*

The box closed on 27 September 1964 when all the trackwork was taken out of use apart from the main running line and a siding to Treskilling china clay works, which closed in 1975. Now only a request stop furnished with a basic hut, the station is passed by Class 50s Nos 50008 *Thunderer* and 50015 *Valiant*

STENALEES: The Goonbarrow branch from Goonbarrow Junction was opened by the CMR on 2 October 1893 serve a number of works in the heart of china clay country. The CMR had been worked by the GWR fro 1 October 1877, but the new line was to be operated by its owners until its whole system was amalgamated wi

the GWR on 1 July 1896. A Pecke 0-6-0ST was purchased to work th branch and was based in a shed Stenalees. Passing the village 13 August 1956, a pair of '160 Class pannier tanks double-hea the 1.00 pm china clay train fro Carbean to Goonbarrow Junctio The long-demolished engine she had been located near to the wat tower visible to the right of th cottages. The train has just passe through the 345-yard Stenalee Tunnel. *Hugh Davies*

The formation in this area is no used as a footpath. Due to th height of the undergrowth, the pr sent view of 20 September 199 was taken further forward to sho the aforementioned cottages. It interesting to note how the skylin has altered with the removal of th clay spoil tips.

GUNHEATH: This rarely photographed location was recorded on a misty 19 June 1956 as a '1600' Class 0-6-0PT indulges in a spot of shunting. The picture was taken from the main line, which approached at a gradient of 1 in 39 and shows New Gunheath siding trailing away to the right. Trains had to reverse here to continue to the terminus at Carbean, and just visible on the extreme left is one rail of this extension. Due to clearance restrictions and track curvature only short-wheelbase engines were allowed over the Goonbarrow branch, and Hawksworth's 1949 design was the last steam class to work the line. *Hugh Davies*

The topography at this location has changed dramatically with continued mining. The houses just visible on the right of the 'past' picture have disappeared and this area now forms part of an enlarged Gunheath pit. A conveyor and road track now mark the approximate route of the railway.

CARBEAN: The final stretch of this 3½-mile branch dropped away sharply, partly at a gradient of 1 in 35. The cramped terminus is depicted on 18 June 1958 as 0-6-0PT No 1626 marshalls its train in the run-round loop. The track runs on to a loading wharf, on which the photographer is standing, whilst a headshunt trails away to the left. *C. H. A. Townley*

The last 2 miles of the branch closed on 29 April 1965, with the section from Wheal Henry (near Goonbarrow Junction) to New Caudledown Siding closing on 3 December 1978. Part of the Carbean site has disappeared into a clay pit, but this 20 September 1992 scene shows that much of the formation can still be traced.

CARBIS: This branch from Bugle was only just over 1 mile long, but served the important Rosemellyn Clay Works and Great Wheal Prosper Clay Kiln; another siding was added in 1912 to serve West Goonbarrow Dries. The terminus is illustrated in July 1960 and shows No 1664 and two GWR 'Toad' brake-vans. The buildings on the left belong to Great Wheal Prosper Dry, whilst the siding on the right served Carbis Wharf where clay and other merchandise was handled. No provision was ever made for run-round facilities and trains always had to be propelled down the line. *Hugh Davies*

Rosemellyn and West Goonbarrow sidings closed in 1948 and 1967 respectively and thereafter traffic only originated from Great Wheal Prosper. The service gradually dwindled from a daily to a weekly train until eventually only a single wagon was dispatched to Scotland monthly. The final such departure occurred on 25 August 1989 and the output is now either taken by lorry or pumped by pipeline to the owners' other railhead at Trelavour, near Nankandillack.

BUGLE. The original Treffry tramway from Ponts' ... terminated at a clay-loading wharf at Molinnis, ... to Bugle. The engine at Bugle worked on to Bugle Wharf, upgraded by the CMR and the line extended for its 1874 opening. At the same time the Carbis branch opened, while another branch from Bugle to Wheal Rose commenced operations in October 1893. The passenger station opened on 20 June 1876 and is pictured on 28 April 1962 as 2-6-2Ts Nos 4564 and 5531 pause with a PRC brake-van tour. Although St Blazey shed closed to steam on that day, these engines and No 5518 were to be stored there as spare until September 1963. *Terry Nicholls*

The Wheal Rose branch formally closed from 29 November 1964, at which date the down loop and up sidings were taken out of use. The line on which the railtour was standing was retained to provide access to the Carbis branch, but has now been lifted. The scene is rather depressing on 25 July 1992 as power cars Nos 43137 and 43007 and the 11.31 Newquay-Paddington pass the island platform. The only surviving through service over a Cornish branch has been operated by HST units on Summer Saturdays since 1988, and they present a somewhat incongruous sight as they trundle along at a maximum 25 mph.

ST DENNIS JUNCTION: Rails first reached this site in 1849 when Treffry opened his tramway from Hendra to Newquay. In 1874 it became an important centre for clay trains with the opening of not only the CMR's Par to Newquay line and the Retew branch to Melangoose Mill, but also the extension of the N&CJR's route from Burngullow. The track to the right of the train is from the Retew branch. The location is seen on 11 July 1955 as 0-6-0PT No 3635 draws away with a train for the reversal of clay trains, that on the left serving the Drinnick/Burngullow line while the right-hand side line

The closure of both the Newquay & Cornwall Junction Railway, a line from Tolcarne and the passing loop on the Newquay branch was used on summer Saturdays until 1986, with the signal box closing in January 1987. More recently the junction has only provided access to engineers' spoil sidings, but these were rarely used and the connection was severed during February 1992 by removing a length of track. On 21 March Class '122' No 55003 passes on the 13.25 Newquay-Par.

89

ST DENNIS & HENDRA: Another of Squire Treffry's horse-drawn tramways was constructed to link Newquay harbour with the developing china clay industry on Hendra Downs. The standard gauge line was opened to St Dennis in 1849 and by 1852 had been extended up an incline plane to Hendra Downs, this section being operated by a stationery engine. When the CMR reconstructed the tramway, the original alignment was used from St Dennis Junction to the foot of the incline, but the route deviated from there on its way to Drinnick. The incline can be noted rising away from the 'new' formation as 'Prairie' tank No 4526 heads towards St Dennis on 1 October 1955 whilst working a PRC brake van special. *Peter Gray*

The line from Parkandillack to St Dennis Junction closed on 6 February 1966, but the trackbed is clearly visible on 20 September 1992. If proposals to divert Newquay trains via Burngullow materialise, this stretch of railway will be restored. The line from St Dennis Junction to Goonbarrow Junction will then close and the section from there to St Blazey will operate as a freight-only siding.

MELEDOR MILL: A branch was opened on 1 June 1874 by the CMR from St Dennis Junction to Melangoose Mill, near the hamlet of Retew. On 1 July 1912 it was extended by the GWR to Meledor Mill and a total length of just over 4 miles, and then in 1929 the railway was further extended a short distance across a road to New Meledor Siding. For most of its route the line followed the course of the River Fal, serving numerous sidings *en route*. The second of the termini possessed two loading platforms and 2-6-2T No 5519 is depicted there on 19 June 1958 as it shunts between them. *David Lawrence*

Traffic over the branch gradually dwindled from the 1960s, with the last load of china clay being carried in about 1980. Most of the track was removed in 1983, but ten years on the platforms are largely intact; the right-hand one is visible behind the nearest post.

ST COLUMB ROAD: Initially named Halloon when the CMR commenced passenger services, this station wa[s] renamed from 1 November 1878 to reflect its position some 2 miles or so from the larger community of St Columb Major. It possessed two platforms and a small goods yard on opening, but the latter had been enlarged by 191[0] and a loading dock constructed. Further alterations to the trackwork took place in 1931-3 when the passing loop was lengthened. The photograph clearly shows the platform-mounted signal box and the main station building which were on the up side. The track on the far right forms part of the goods yard. *Lens of Sutton*

The signal box closed on 3 January 1965 when the passing loop and all of the sidings were taken out of use. Only a small hut now provides shelter for intending passengers and this can be noted to the rear of Class '153' N[o] 153377 as it departs with the 14.40 Par-Newquay on 23 December 1992.

TOLCARN JUNCTION: Originally known as Treloggan Junction when it connected the Newquay to Hendra tramway with the East Wheal Rose branch, it was renamed Newquay Junction on the opening of the CMR. When the Newquay branch was re-aligned prior to the arrival of the railway from Chacewater, the junction was given its third and final name. It is pictured here on 28 April 1962 as 2-6-2Ts Nos 4564 and 5531 are watered whilst working the PRC brake-van tour already pictured. The two lines on the left of the engines are carriage sidings, whilst the Newquay to Par branch (this section doubled in about 1940) and a further siding are visible in the background. A signal box stood just out of view to the right, whilst a third spur of the triangle also existed. This east curve had closed in 1888 but was reinstated in 1931 to allow the turning of locomotives. *Terry Nicholls*

Both the east and west chords were taken out of use in October 1963, while the remaining section of the Newquay branch was singled and the signal box closed on 23 November 1964. An industrial estate now covers much of the site, but careful study of the 16 October 1992 view reveals single unit No 153318 on the 16.25 Newquay-Par crossing from left to right in the background.

NEWQUAY: Attempts to develop the harbour here were largely unsuccessful as it suffered in comparison with th
south coast ports due to its cramped facilities and position on the inhospitable Atlantic coast. However, the com
ing of the railway helped to transform Newquay from a small fishing and trading port into Cornwall's premier hol
iday resort. As the tourist trade developed, the GWR extended the station and facilities to meet the demand
Traffic reached a peak in the 1950s, but with mass car ownership the situation was to change rapidly. The 'pas
view was taken as recently as Sunday 4 October 1987 and shows one of the unsuccessful 'Skipper' units, N
142025, after arrival with the 15.0
from Par. *David Mitchell*

Much of the trackwork in th
area had already been lifted b
then, but that weekend als
marked a further rationalisation o
facilities. The final scheduled loco
motive-hauled train had departe
the previous day, and the signa
box was to close with only a singl
platform in use on the Monday
Although HST units still visit o
summer Saturdays, the station i
unmanned and presents a sad pic
ture with the truncated trackwor
and buildings either let or demol
ished.

TREWERRY & TRERICE HALT: The Newquay to Chacewater line was constructed in several parts, with the section from Tolcarn Junction near the village of Newlyn East originally forming a branch to Treffry's Newquay tramway. This opened on 26 February 1849 to transport lead and silver ore from East Wheal Rose mine. After being taken over by the CMR, the railway was reconstructed and extended to Treamble. Finally, on 2 January 1905 this section was opened to passengers when the Chacewater - Perranporth branch was extended by the GWR. Trewerry & Trerice Halt opened on 14 August of that year and was located adjacent to Trewerry Mill. *Lens of Sutton*

Since closure a house has been built on the site with its garage standing where the track once ran. However, a section of the halt survives in the garden, complete with one of the lamp-posts.

It is also pleasing to report that half a mile south of here there has been a railway revival. On 16 June 1974 a 15-inch gauge line commenced operations over about a mile of the branch formation from Benny Mill to a leisure complex at East Wheal Rose. The Lappa Valley is therefore the fourth railway to run over this route. Berwyn 0-6-0 *Muffin* awaits its 11.50 departure from Benny Halt on 16 October 1992.

MITCHELL & NEWLYN HALT was one of six halts opened on this branch on 14 August 1905, and served two v
lages, although being rather inconvenient for both. Originally of timber construction, the halt was later rebuilt
concrete and provided with a primitive corrugated iron shelter. Located on an embankment and somewh
exposed to the elements, one can imagine that on occasions it must have been an unpleasant experience waiti
for a train! *Lens of Sutton*

No doubt due to its isolated position the halt today is remarkably intact and can be reached via its original fo
path. The turbines belonging to one of Cornwall's wind farms stand on an adjacent hill, the technology from tv
different centuries providing an interesting contrast.

SHEPHERDS: The CMR opened its route to Treamble Mill and Gravel Hill with the rest of its network in 1874. Serving an iron ore mining area, a downturn in the industry led to the closure of the Gravel Hill extension in 1888. When the branch from Chacewater was constructed, it joined the mineral railway near two old mines named Shepherds, and the junction station was given that name. One of three passing places on the new line, the station possessed a signal box, two platforms and a small goods yard. The Treamble line closed in 1917 and the rails were sent to France as part of the war effort. Surprisingly, an upturn in business led to the reinstatement of this route in 1926, and traffic was to continue until 1949, albeit intermittently in later years. On 7 August 1961 0-6-0PT No 3709 pauses in Shepherds station with a train for Newquay. The Treamble line formerly trailed in to the right of this scene. *Rodney Lissenden*

A visit on 16 October 1992 revealed that the site now forms part of a farmyard although the iron railings on the left, next to the van, are reminders of the past. The trackbed can be traced beyond the tractor.

MITHIAN HALT. The next stations on the line were Goonhavern Halt and Perranporth. The latter was the most important intermediate stop on the route, its sandy beach an attraction for the growing holiday trade. Indeed, traffic increased sufficiently to warrant the opening of Perranporth Beach Halt on 20 July 1931. To the west of the main station and crossing place, it was conveniently sited nearer the beach and town centre.

About 2 miles further on the hamlet of Mithian was also provided with its own station. On 11 July 1961 '5700' Class 0-6-0PT No 7715 passes the single platform with the 11.00 am Newquay-Truro. *Peter Gray*

The cutting has been completely filled in here and a builders yard now occupies the site. All signs of the overbridge from which the past photograph was taken have disappeared, but the parapets of the bridge visible behind the train still survive.

GOONBELL HALT: Situated in a cutting and serving an adjacent hamlet of the same name, this was a typical GWR Halt complete with its pagoda-style shelter. On 11 July 1961 '4575' Class 2-6-2T No 5562 drifts into the station with the 11.50 am Newquay-Truro. *Peter Gray*

Since closure of the line on 4 February 1963, the cutting has been infilled and the land amalgamated with an adjoining field. A single parapet survives from the bridge from which the 'past' picture was taken, the author also looking over it to take this 23 December 1992 photograph. Some original fencing survives to the left of the scene.

ST AGNES: One of the two original stations when the line opened as far as Perranporth on 6 July 1903, this ser
a large village and was one of the branch's more important stops. Initially there was only a single platform,
the layout was altered and an island platform and passing loop provided from 4 July 1937. Twenty-four ye
later, on 10 July 1961, '5700' Class 0-6-0PT No 3709 heads away from St Agnes on the 3.20 pm Newquay-Truro.
station is located in the left distance. *Peter Gray*

The ground south of the overbridge has now been levelled, but the cutting does still survive on the other si
The main station building also exists as part of an industrial development known as the Great Western Railw
Yard. The railway connection is further enhanced by the display of an ex-Devonport Dockyard diesel shunter n
the entrance.

UNT HAWKE HALT: Another of the halts to be opened on 14 August 1905, this was rather rather inconvenient-
ated about a mile from its namesake village. Approximately half a mile north of the halt, and adjacent to Gover
n, pannier tank No 3709 heads the 4.39 pm Chacewater-Newquay on 10 July 1961. *Peter Gray*

farm track now follows the
te of the railway. Reference
its to look for in this 27 August
2 view are the gate-post on the
and the fencing on the right. It
different story immediately
ind the camera, however, as
formation has been totally
milated into a field.

ST AUSTELL (1): The main line reached here in 1859 when the Cornwall Railway opened, and the town gre[w]
importance, not least due to its role as the commercial and administrative centre of the china clay industr[y]
growth in both passenger and goods traffic led to an expansion in facilities over the years, particularly when
existing sidings in the station area were inadequate and a new goods yard was provided to the east, opening [in]
November 1931. 'Large Prairie' tank No 5148 is depicted here passing the entrance to the yard with a down g[oods]
on 12 May 1951. The line on the left is the up and down loop which ran as far as the station, while the hut ho[uses]
a ground frame. *John Bamsey*

Traffic to the depot, particularly in coal, lasted into the 1980s, but since closure the track in the yard has [been]
lifted although the loop line is still in situ. The 10.35 Paddington-Penzance HST approaches on 7 February 199[3]

AUSTELL (2): The town was also the starting point of one of Cornwall's earliest railways. Constructed to trans-
t clay to its harbour, the 4-mile-long Pentewan Railway was built to a gauge of 2 ft 6 in and opened in 1829.
ginally horse-drawn, locomotives were introduced in 1873, but recurrent silting of the harbour and the failure
he railway to penetrate into the clay-producing areas led to its closure in 1918. St Austell's attractive station is
tured here on 20 February 1973 as Class '52' No D1042 *Western Princess* waits for the road with 4M07, the
05 Ponsandane-Manchester, comprising a single conflat loaded with broccoli. The siding on the right of the
n was used for motorail services. *David Mitchell*

lthough St Austell is still an important passenger railhead, the motorail trains no longer run and remaining
ight traffic passes by. On 28
tember 1992 No 37671 *Tre Pol*
en is on a Crugwallins (north of
ngullow) to Carne Point work-
. The sidings have been truncat-
and the semaphore signals were
oved in late 1979, this stretch
ine now coming under the con-
of Par signal box.

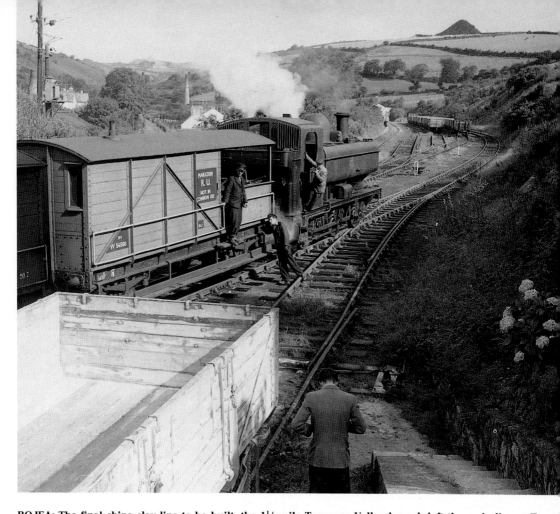

BOJEA: The final china clay line to be built, the 1¹/₂-mile Trenance Valley branch left the main line at Trena
Junction, west of St Austell. Construction began in 1913, but work was interrupted by the First World War,
the first section to Bojea sidings was not opened until 1 May 1920. The line was known to local railwaymen as

Bojea branch. The sidings are s
here on 13 August 1956 as a '5?
Class 0-6-0PT commences shun
operations, having just arri
with the 9.15 am goods from
Austell. The whitened clay wa
in the foreground is on the Carl
Farm or Loverings Siding wh
served adjacent clay dries. *H*
Davies

The two tracks on the left of
yard and the Carlyon Farm Sid
were all taken out of use on 27 J
1964 and lifted soon afterwa
Traffic continued over part of
branch until 1968, latterly ope
ed by a Class '08' diesel shun
stabled at St Austell. The far en
the site is now a fuel depot,
much of it is now heavily ov
grown, as was discovered on
September 1992. The spoil tip
the distant hillside is the best I
between the two pictures.

NSALSON: The Trenance Valley
nch was extended to here, with
ffic commencing on 24 May
0. Located just to the south of
terminus were sidings serving
kell China Clay Works, and 2-6-2T
4552 was photographed while
nting these in the 1950s. The
in' line from Bojea runs in from
left. *David Lawrence*

he branch north of Boskell was
sed on 27 July 1964, and com-
tely on 6 May 1968. The siding
a has disappeared in the under-
wth, but a rough trail follows
ne of the branch formation. A lit-
further south of here were sid-
s known as Lower Ruddle Yard
d some track can still be traced
either side of the loading dock.
hose wishing to learn more
out the china clay industry should
it the Wheal Martyn museum,
rth of the site of Lansalson yard.

TRENANCE SIDINGS: Back on the main line, and located north of the line between St Austell and Gover viadu[...] these sidings served the coal-fired Trenance clay dries. The track layout was modified in 1899 when the main l[ine] from Burngullow to St Austell was doubled, and a new signal box was also opened, replacing an earlier insta[lla-]tion situated a little further to the east. The 'new' box can just be seen on the right of this 20 June 1956 scene a[s St] Blazey's '4300' Class 2-6-0 No 6305 passes with a down goods. *Hugh Davies*

The signal box and sidings closed on 25 September 1966 and much of the site is now hidden in the und[er-]growth. On 20 September 1992 a Class '153' unit and Class '158' No 158827 pass by forming the 7.35 Bris[tol-]Penzance.

BURNGULLOW: A little over 2 miles to the west of St Austell, the Cornwall Railway opened a station here on 1 February 1863. It had a single platform on what is now the down side, and due to the presence of clay dries and sidings on the other side of the line, it was not possible to build a second platform following the doubling of the main line in 1898-9. The station was therefore resited to the west, with the down platform located opposite the junction with the Newquay & Cornwall Junction Railway and the shorter up platform between the main and branch lines. The new station opened on 1 August 1901, but was only to last until 14 September 1931. A surviving building on the up side can be noted as Class '37' No 37267 eases off the branch on 28 September 1978 with a train of loaded clay hoods. *David Mitchell*

The main line was singled on 5 October 1986 when the down line was taken out between Burngullow and Probus. The 1901-vintage signal box was closed at the same time, but still stands for the use of permanent way staff. On 4 May 1991 Class '50' No 50015 *Valiant* returns from Drinnick Mill with Pathfinder Tours' 'Cornish Centurion II'. The rough track in the foreground marks the site of the former down platform.

LANJETH: The broad gauge Newquay & Cornwall Junction Railway was built to provide access to the many cl[a]
pits north of St Austell, and was planned to link the CR main line with the Treffry tramway near St Denni[s]
However, funds only allowed construction as far as Drinnick Mill, with the line opening on 1 July 1869. The ra[il]
way was later transferred to the standard gauge CMR, which completed the link in 1874. However, there was to [be]
a break of gauge at Drinnick until the abolition of the broad gauge in 1892. A dispute between the GWR a[nd]
Carpella United Clay Co as to mineral rights under the railway led to closure of part of the line in 1909, and th[is]
'Carpella Break' was to last until 1922 when a deviation from the original route opened.

Lanjeth crossing is located about a mile up the branch. On 13 July 1961 0-6-0PTs Nos 9755 and 1624 head aw[ay] from the crossing with a china cl[ay] train. *Peter Gray*

This has always been a freigh[t] only line, but if the Newqua[y] branch diversion proposals ev[er] materialise it will receive its fir[st] regular passenger service. In th[e] meantime it still serves its origin[al] purpose, and on 12 October 19[9?] Class '37' No 37412 hauls fo[ur] Polybulk tanks from Drinnick M[ill] towards Burngullow where it wi[ll] add another five wagons befo[re] heading for St Blazey yard.

GRAMPOUND ROAD: Opened to serve a widespread agricultural district, the station also acted as a railhead for Newquay before passenger trains ran to the resort, a horse-bus providing the link. On 7 July 1955 'Hall' Class 4-6-0 No 6911 *Holker Hall* passes by with the 11.00 Penzance-Paddington. Two goods sidings are positioned on the left, while the goods shed can be observed on the up side behind the front coaches and the signal box can just be spotted on the up platform behind the fourth vehicle. *R. C. Riley*

All the sidings and the crossover were taken out of use on 19 September 1964, and the station closed from 5 October, one of six on the Cornish main line to lose their passenger service that day. The signal box closed on 2 June 1972, but the goods shed still stands in commercial use. Plasser and Theurer tamping machine No 73415 passes over the single track on 16 October 1992.

PROBUS & LADOCK PLATFORM: Situated about 2 miles west of Grampound Road, this halt was opened on February 1908. The platforms were largely of wooden construction, but at the east end surviving evidence su gests that these sections were brick built. Corrugated iron shelters were provided on each side, as can be seen i this 7 July 1955 view. Serving an agricultural area, it would appear that there must have been a healthy trade i rabbits, as photographer R. C. Riley recalls being told that it was closed because of myxamatosis! *R. C. Riley*

Closure actually came on 2 December 1957 and a signalling relay room now marks the location. The line ha become double track again just east of here. The concrete bunker on the left serves as a reference point whe comparing the two views.

RURO (1): The West Cornwall Railway was the first to reach the county's only cathedral town, but the present-day station dates from 11 May 1859 and the opening of the Cornwall Railway. Already an important commercial centre, the arrival of the railway helped Truro to grow in prosperity. The original cramped station was rebuilt, with work completed in 1900. The new platform 4 was used for up main line trains such as the up 'Cornish Riviera', which on 1 May 1959 (the station's centenary) was hauled by 4-6-0 No 6850 *Cleeve Grange*. *Michael Mensing*

This former through line was converted to a siding on 7 May 1971, with all up trains then using platform 3. The siding was subsequently shortened in 1974 and a building erected where the 'Grange' had once stood, although this has since been removed. The through goods lines survived until 1988. The present view has been taken from a slightly different angle to include the only surviving signal box in the area, formerly known as Truro East. Class '158' No 158838 approaches on the 9.10 Plymouth-Penzance.

TRURO (2): On Saturday 16 May 1959 '45xx' 2-6-2T No 5500 with the 9.12 am from Newquay enters platform 3, which was normally used by Falmouth and Newquay branch services. Truro West signal box can be observed, with the engine shed behind it. The lines to the right lead to the large goods yard. *Michael Mensing*

The signal box closed on 7 November 1971 and has been demolished, and many of the sidings were taken out of use at the same time. The rationalised scene is apparent on 25 August 1992 as Class '47' No 47463 approaches at the head of the 12.15 Penzance to Paddington Mail.

PENWTHERS JUNCTION: This splendid 11 July 1961 view from above Highertown Tunnel includes no fewer than three trains travelling to or from different branch lines. On the left, No 5537 waits to leave the Newham branch with a goods train, while in the background a DMU forms a Truro to Falmouth service. In the meantime 0-6-0PT No 9635 approaches the tunnel with the 9.12 am Newquay to Truro via Chacewater. When the standard gauge West Cornwall reached Truro in 1852 its terminus was located close to this junction and named Truro Road. The station closed on 16 April 1855 following the extension to Newham. The tunnel was dug to connect with the broad gauge Cornwall Railway, and from 1866 mixed gauge running was introduced westwards as required by statute. *Peter Gray*

The junction was rationalised on 7 November 1971 when the Newham branch was taken out of use, the signal box closed and two-way running for Falmouth trains introduced over the down main line from Truro station. On 25 August 1992 Class '108' DMU No 954 approaches on the 10.25 Penzance-Plymouth.

NEWHAM (1): In 1855 the West Cornwall Railway opened a $2^1/_2$-mile extension to Newham on the banks of the Truro River. For a period of four years the terminus was the town's only station, then on the arrival of the Cornwall Railway most trains were diverted to the new Truro station and passenger services to Newham were only to last until 16 September 1863. The line then settled down to life as a freight-only branch. On 11 July 1961 '4575' Class 2-6-2T No 5537 is depicted climbing away from Newham. *Peter Gray*

Much of the formation is now used as a footpath, as illustrated in August 1992.

NEWHAM (2): The wharf is seen on 20 July 1960 as 'Prairie' tank No 5552 shunts the sidings; note Truro cathedral prominent on the skyline. The original timber-built terminus with its overall roof is located in the distance behind the wagons. Truro River is on the right. *R. C. Riley*

The branch finally closed on 7 November 1971, and this area now forms part of an industrial estate. The towers and spires of the Victorian cathedral still dominate the horizon.

PERRANWELL: The Cornwall Railway opened its branch to Falmouth on 24 August 1863. A single-track broad gauge route, the line was heavily engineered and featured two tunnels and no fewer than eight of Brunel's timber viaducts. Between 1923 and 1934 four of these were replaced by embankments, and masonry viaducts were constructed in place of the others. One of the two original intermediate stations, Perranwell had two platforms and a passing loop. The main building was of granite construction and located on the down side. Its most notable asset however, was a splendid elevated signal box which straddled a siding between the goods shed and the down platform. On 20 May 1959 2-6-2T No 5500 waits to leave with a pick-up goods after depositing a single wagon in the yard. *Michael Mensing*

The down sidings were closed in 1965, and the signal box closed on 18 April 1966 when the crossing loop was taken out of use. The goods yard and surviving shed are now occupied by a firm of scaffolders.

PENRYN: The other original inter-mediate station was rebuilt in 1923 when Penryn viaduct was replaced by an embankment and the track realigned. This town had a good deal of industrial activity, including mills and an iron foundry, and a sizeable goods yard was provided by the railway. The yard's headshunt is seen on the left here as 'Prairie' tank No 5562 climbs towards the station with the 5.05 pm Falmouth-Truro on 10 May 1959. *Michael Mensing*

The goods yard, passing loop and signal box were all taken out of use on 7 November 1971. Just a single line passes through what is now a simple unstaffed halt. On 25 August 1992 Class '153' No 153362 approaches on the 11.55 Falmouth-Truro.

FALMOUTH: The branch terminus is viewed to advantage on 17 May 1959 as '4575' Class No 5500 arrives with the 12.03 from Truro (the 10.50 from Newquay). The impressive goods shed is on the left, while out of sight behind the platform a line runs down to the docks. Originally it was planned that the terminus would be sited nearer the town centre, but with the opening of the docks it was decided to route the railway around the west side of Falmouth to this location above the port, in anticipation of the traffic that would develop. *Michael Mensing*

The track layout was rationalised in 1966 following closure of the signal box, and the platform was shortened on 19 March 1969. The station closed in 1970 and was replaced by a new halt about half a mile away and nearer the centre of the town. However, the original terminus reopened on 5 May 1975; now known as Falmouth Docks, the truncated platform again [...]

CHACEWATER (1) opened on 25 August 1852 when the West Cornwall Railway was extended from Redruth
Truro Road. It subsequently led a quiet existence serving its namesake town about a mile away, until in 190:
became the junction for the branch which initially opened as far as Perranporth on 6 July. A loop and island pl
form were built in 1912 for branch trains, and these were photographed from a down train on 8 April 1960 as 2-6
No 5515 waits with a Newquay train. *R. C. Riley*

The branch closed in 1963 and, having lost its main role, the station was only to remain open until 5 Octol
1964. Although evidence of the down platform remains today, only a bank of grass and rubble marks the site
the former island platform.

CEWATER (2): Originally branch trains to Newquay travelled over the main line for the short journey to the gular Blackwater Junction. However, from 9 November 1924 an independent line was opened parallel to main line, with the physical connection at the junction removed and its signal box closed. The west curve at unction had been an earlier casualty, closing on 5 May 1919 having been rendered largely redundant since essation of through passenger traffic from the west on to the branch. At 12.11 pm on 6 August 1961 North sh Type 2 diesel-hydraulic No 5 leaves Chacewater on the ' line with the 11.40 am from o. *Ron Lumber*

e goods yard remained open 1987 to serve a cement distri- on point, but the connection the main line was not taken until September 1992. On 23 mber a Class '153/158' combi- on passes on the 12.40 zance-Plymouth. The yard is occupied as a milk depot.

SCORRIER: The first mineral railway to be built in Cornwall was the Poldice to Portreath Tramroad. This h[orse?] drawn line of about 4 feet gauge was built to link copper mines in the Scorrier and St Day areas with the ha[rbour] at Portreath. The first rail was laid in 1809 and the section from Portreath to Scorrier House was in use by 1[...] with the whole line open by early in 1819. As the mines became exhausted, traffic dwindled and the route fi[nally] closed in the 1860s. By then another railway had reached Scorrier with the extension of the West Cor[nwall]

Railway in 1852. A station opened and was known as Sco[rrier] Gate until 1856. It reverted to [old] name in 1859 before the f[inal] renaming in 1896. Scorrier app[ears] to have been a rarely [pho]tographed location, but this [view] from the 1950s does show [the] down platform and buildin[g to] advantage. *David Lawrence*

The station closed fro[m 5] October 1964, and only the c[rum]bling platform survives today.

REDRUTH OLD GOODS YARD: The Hayle Railway was built as a standard gauge mineral line to convey ore from mining areas to the port and foundry at Hayle. An extension from Portreath Junction to Redruth opened on 11 June 1838, and shortly afterwards a branch was opened from Redruth Junction, just short of the eastern terminus,

Tresavean to serve the extensive mining district around Gwennap. Passenger services were introduced from Hayle to Redruth from 25 May 1843 by attaching coaches to the rear of goods trains, then the Hayle railway closed in 1852 for reconstruction as part of the West Cornwall Railway. This opened from Redruth to Penzance on 11 March with the former place now served by a new station in a different location. The former terminus was relegated to life as a goods yard connected by a spur to the new main line. This rare view shows how it looked in June 1958.

J. A. Townley

Some of the track was removed in 1960, with the rest lifted on 14 February 1968. The current photo was taken on 23 December 1992 from a position a little further forward, and shows that most of the site is now used as a car park.

CAMBORNE: After leaving Redruth, the main line passes the site of Carn Brea station which closed in 1961, which had been the location of the West Cornwall Railway's workshops. The whole of this area once saw int[e] tin and copper mining activity and evidence in the shape of old engine houses can be seen from the passing tr[a] Redruth and Camborne merge to form the largest urban district in the county, but each place retains its sep[a] identity and station. On 7 July 1955 4-6-0 No 6931 *Aldborough Hall* pauses at the short down platform with a [s] per for Penzance. The rails on the right lead to sidings and the goods shed, which were behind the photograp[h] *R. C. Riley*

All the sidings were taken out of use on 28 May 1965 and since their removal the down platform has b[een] lengthened; close examination of the February 1993 scene reveals the lighter coloured brickwork of the ex[ten] sion. The goods shed still stands, now in commercial use. The station is unmanned for part of the time and [only?] basic huts are provided on each platform for shelter. There have been recent suggestions that Camborne [and] Redruth stations should close and be replaced by a new facility at Carn Brea.

INEAR ROAD (1) opened in 1843 when the passenger service over the Hayle Railway commenced. Built to
ve a number of rural communities, it grew in importance when it became the junction for the Helston branch,
ch opened on 9 May 1887. The site was subsequently developed with goods yards at each end of the layout.
ange' 4-6-0 No 6837 *Forthampton Grange* runs into the station at 7.20 pm on 18 July 1959, with what is proba-
the 11.05 am Paddington to Penzance. A sizeable marshalling yard can be noted behind the rear of the train,
lst the Helston branch disappears beneath the overbridge in the middle distance. *Peter Gray*
he station closed from 5 October 1964, the day after goods services over the branch ceased. Over the next 12
nths all the sidings were taken out of use and both of the signal boxes were closed. The level crossing is now
tected by automatic barriers which are seen in operation on 16 October 1992 as HST power car No 43009
ds the 10.35 Paddington-Penzance.

GWINEAR ROAD (2): The Helston branch left Gwinear Road on a straight alignment, whereas the east yard the main line to Camborne curved away sharply to the north-east. Here we see '4500' Class 2-6-2T No 4549 lea on 10 July 1961 with the 11.55 am to Helston. *Peter Gray*

The branch formation has now disappeared into a field and it is difficult to imagine the scale of activity could once be seen here. The same viewpoint today does, however, provide a clearer sight of the main line c ing away. On 27 August 1992 an HST set speeds by on the 16.30 Penzance to Paddington service.

AZE was the first station down
Helston branch. Serving the vil-
e of Praze-an-Beeble, this station
d a single platform with a sub-
ntial building of stone construc-
n. At one time there was a loop
trolled by a ground frame, but
e connection was taken out in
out 1950 leaving a siding facing
ards Gwinear Road. This attrac-
e scene was recorded on 11 July
1. *Peter Gray*

ince closure all trace of the sta-
n has disappeared and a
elling erected on the site. The
kground trees are the best ref-
nce points when comparing the
scenes.

NANCEGOLLAN: 'Prairie' tank No 4549 approaches the station on 11 July 1961 with a Helston to Gwinear R
train. In a fertile area, this location saw considerable goods traffic, particularly in agricultural produce, and fa
ties were expanded to meet demand. Originally only possessing one platform with a passing loop and a single
ing, the station was rebuilt in 1937 when two platforms were provided and a sizeable yard laid. *Peter Gray*

Industrial units now stand on the station site. The bushes in the middle of the August 1992 view mark the ro
of the railway.

UTHALL HALT: Opened on 1 July 1905, the short platform was of timber construction with a 'pagoda' hut pro-
ded for shelter. It was officially designated Truthall Platform in 1906, but always seemed to have actually borne
original name. On 15 July 1961 2-6-2T No 4588 with the 2.25 pm from Gwinear Road slows to pick up two pas-
gers for Helston. Soon after leaving the halt the train will cross the 373-yard-long granite Cober Viaduct, which
s the most notable engineering feature on the branch. *Peter Gray*
The line closed to passengers on 3 November 1962, although the goods service lasted for almost a further two
ars. In the period since then the site of this halt has become totally overgrown.

HELSTON: It was originally hoped that the railway would be extended through the Lizard peninsula, and the t[...]
minus here was therefore built as a through station. Instead, however, on 17 August 1903 the GWR introduced [...]
pioneering omnibus service from Helston to The Lizard, and any such thoughts were soon forgotten. Britai[...]
most southerly terminus was recorded on 21 July 1957 as 2-6-2T No 4505 engages in shunting activity. The sin[...]
platform is largely hidden behind the signal box whilst the substantial goods shed is partially obscured by stea[...]
The spur in the foreground leads to the single-road engine shed. *Peter Gray*

Most of the site has now been taken over by housing, but Station Road still retains its name although it is n[...]
on a slightly different alignment. The goods shed survives and has been converted into a social club as part o[...]
residential development, and can be seen to the right of this 26 August 1992 scene. A section of the platform ed[...]
is also in situ.

HAYLE (1): The Hayle Railway included an inclined plane in its route from Gwinear to Hayle, and the West Cornwall Railway had to introduce a significant deviation to avoid this Angarrack Incline when it reconstructed the line in 1852. Hayle was important both for its foundry and, more particularly, as a port for the transport of mining ore. A station was opened by the new railway, comprising two platforms and a passing loop with single sidings on each side. The layout was to change slightly over the years, particularly when the main line was doubled. The station is pictured from the footbridge on 18 June 1962 as Class '22' No D6315 arrives on a Penzance topper. The delightful signal box dated from 1912 when it replaced two earlier installations. *R. C. Riley*

Latterly only used to control access to the Wharves branch, the signal box finally closed in 1982 and has been demolished along with the station buildings; only basic huts are now provided on each side. The footbridge has also gone and passengers now cross the tracks via a boarded crossing. Class '101' No 879 calls on 27 August 1992 with the 12.40 Plymouth-Penzance.

HAYLE (2): In another view from further along the footbridge, the sidings north of the station are seen on 10 April 1959 as an unidentified '57xx' 0-6-0PT shunts its train. An engine shed once stood on this site but was closed in 1918. The sidings date from the early years of this century, while the branch to the wharves starts its descent on the left. *Hugh Davies*

The yard was lifted in the 1966-70 period and housing has been built on the far end of the site. As can be seen in this 16 October 1992 view, the rest is a wasteland with only the hut hinting at the activity that could once be witnessed here.

HAYLE WHARVES: The Hayle Railway had terminated at the quayside, whereas the more elevated route of the West Cornwall Railway meant that that line crossed the port area by a viaduct. It was originally intended to install a wagon lift from this viaduct to connect with the sidings below, but instead a branch was constructed. Opened on 11 March 1852, the line was heavily graded and featured one of the first sand drags to stop runaway trains. Latterly the main traffic over the branch was oil and coal. On 26 July 1979 Class '25' No 25057 crosses the main A30 road before attacking the 1 in 30 climb to Hayle station. *David Mitchell*

Traffic ceased in early 1981, and the track was lifted in the following year. Today the trackbed is used by local people as a footpath.

ST ERTH station opened with the West Cornwall Railway in 1852, when it was known as St Ives Road. It was rebuilt in 1876 and renamed on 1 June 1877 when the branch to St Ives was opened. Further remodelling occurred at the end of the century when first a crossing loop and down main platform were added, then subsequently the main line was doubled to Hayle. A bay platform was provided for branch services and this is illustrated at 2.04 pm on 30 August 1958 as 2-6-2T No 4563 arrives from St Ives. A creamery is located out of the picture to the left; for many years this generated substantial traffic for the railway. *Peter Gray*

Since 1980 milk is no longer conveyed by rail, and many of the sidings at St Erth have been removed. However the station is still largely intact and retains much of its character, particularly as the signal box survives and controls semaphore signalling. Happily the branch also continues to provide a valuable service. On 23 December 1992 Class '122' Nos 55003 and 55009 arrive on the 14.20 from St Ives.

LELANT: The line to St Ives was the last broad gauge branch to be built, but mixed gauge operation was introduced from St Erth to Lelant Quay in October 1888. The station building was of timber construction and can just be seen on 9 September 1961 as No 4563 arrives with the 9.55 am from St Ives. The line to the quay formerly curved away out of the picture to the right on an embankment, but closed early this century. *Peter Gray*

The station building has been extended and is now a private dwelling, its occupiers enjoying this picturesque setting adjacent to the Hayle estuary. Trains still stop here, but the service is not so frequent since the opening of Lelant Saltings station on 27 May 1978. Sited a quarter of a mile or so south of here, it was opened as part of a 'park and ride' scheme and has proved to be very successful. In the summer of 1992 one train to call here was the 14.05 St Ives to St Erth, and on 27 August it comprised Class '101' No 824 and Class '122' Nos 55012 and 55009, the formation strengthened to cater for the extra business generated by the visit of the 'Radio One Roadshow' to St Ives.

ST IVES SHED: Although only 4¼ miles long, the St Ives branch is heavily engineered and provides spectacular views of St Ives Bay as it hugs the coastline. The terminus was constructed on land cut into the cliffside overlooking Porthminster beach, and a single-road stone-built engine shed was provided to the south of the station. A sub-

shed to Penzance, it can be seen on the left in this 25 August 1958 view as 'Prairie' tank No 4563 departs for St Erth. The train has just crossed a 106-yard-long viaduct. *Terry Nicholls*

The shed closed in September 1961 when branch services were dieselised, and the site is now overgrown as recorded on 26 August 1992 as Class '101' No 824 and Class '122' No 55012 pass on the 18.55 St Ives-St Erth.

ST IVES: Historically a fishing port, the arrival of the railway initially benefited this industry. However, it was to play an even greater role in developing the town as a major holiday resort. The cramped terminus was to see an intensive service including the running of through Paddington trains at the height of the summer season. Class '4500' 2-6-2T No 4563 is illustrated shortly before departure on 25 August 1958. The path on the right leads down to the beach. *Terry Nicholls*

The rapid growth in car ownership deprived the branch of much traffic and it was listed for closure in the Beeching Report. Fortunately it was to survive, although not without a rationalisation of the facilities provided. In particular the original station was demolished in 1971 to make way for a car park, and a new concrete platform was erected to the left of these views on the alignment of the former goods yard. St Ives's narrow streets are unsuited to road traffic and access is regulated in the summer, which hopefully should secure the future of this branch line in years to come.

LONG ROCK: Sited about a mile east of the terminus, Penzance's engine shed was opened in 1914 when it replaced an earlier depot located adjacent to the station. The new facility comprised a four-road shed with associated workshops, coaling stage and turntable. The main building can be glimpsed on the right on 11 May 1959 as 4-6-0 No 6875 *Hindford Grange* passes on the 1.55 pm Penzance-Plymouth. Visible above the rear of the train is the large goods shed at Ponsandane which opened in December 1937. *Michael Mensing*

Single-line working was introduced over the main line west of Marazion in 1974. The shed had closed to steam in September 1962 but continued to stable diesels until 1976. Subsequently the buildings were demolished and the site cleared before a new HST depot was constructed thereon. These units took over the 'Golden Hind' and 'Cornish Riviera Express' from 6 August 1979 and now operate most InterCity services in the Duchy.

Locomotive-hauled passenger services are almost a thing of the past, but during the summer of 1992 the engine and seating coaches of the 'Night Riviera' sleeper were used to allow the release of a Class '158' elsewhere. On 26 August Class '47' No 47818 heads eastwards along the shores of Mounts Bay with the 12.20 Penzance-Plymouth. The goods yard at Ponsandane by the side of a moorman's hut on the right

142

PENZANCE: The original West Cornwall terminus was very cramped and a new station was opened by the GWR in 1879, with further improvements being made following the abolition of the broad gauge. However, even these were to prove inadequate, and from 1937 the site was enlarged by claiming land from the sea and the station was rebuilt, with goods facilities moved to the new depot at Ponsandane. Mainland Britain's most westerly terminus is pictured here on 12 July 1956. *R. C. Riley*

The semaphore signalling was replaced in 1982 and the sidings on the far left have disappeared. Otherwise from this angle the station still looks much as it did before, particularly with the replacement of the overall roof in 1990 at a cost of £200,000. On the left of this 25 August 1992 view Class '47' No 47471 awaits departure with the 9.30 TPO to Leeds, whilst on the right No 47802 stands with the stock of the 'Night Riviera' sleeper which will leave for Paddington at 22.15.

Penzance is the end of the line for our journey through the Duchy, and this final photograph (*above*) shows the end of the line for steam working over the Cornish main line. On 3 May 1964 a crowd gathers around 'West Country' 4-6-2 No 34002 *Salisbury* which has arrived with the 'Cornubian' railtour. It is fascinating to study the detail in this picture; note the board in the foreground which reveals that a car and its driver could travel to Paddington by motorail for the princely sum of £8 17s 6d! *Hugh Ballantyne*

INDEX OF LOCATIONS